Windharp

Windharp

Poems of Ireland since 1916

edited by
Niall MacMonagle

PENGUIN
IRELAND

PENGUIN IRELAND

UK | USA | Canada | Ireland | Australia
India | New Zealand | South Africa

Penguin Ireland is part of the Penguin Random House group of companies
whose addresses can be found at global.penguinrandomhouse.com.

First published 2015
001
Editorial matter copyright © Niall MacMonagle, 2015
The Acknowledgements on pages 297–310 constitute an extension of this copyright page

Typeset in Minion Pro by Palimpsest Book Production Limited, Falkirk, Stirlingshire
Printed in Great Britain by Clays Ltd, St Ives plc
A CIP catalogue record for this book is available from the British Library

ISBN : 978-1-844-88318-9

www.greenpenguin.co.uk

Penguin Random House is committed to a
sustainable future for our business, our readers
and our planet. This book is made from Forest
Stewardship Council® certified paper.

In memory of Seamus Heaney

For his bounty

There was no winter in't . . .

Contents

Introduction xv

The Wayfarer PATRICK PEARSE 1

Lament for Thomas MACDONAGH FRANCIS LEDWIDGE 3

Easter 1916 W. B. YEATS 4

To My Daughter Betty, The Gift of God
   THOMAS KETTLE 8

The Long Vacation KATHARINE TYNAN 10

Comrades EVA GORE-BOOTH 11

Sixteen Dead Men DORA SIGERSON SHORTER 12

The Six Who Were Hanged THOMAS MACGREEVY 14

The Lost Heifer AUSTIN CLARKE 18

The Stare's Nest by My Window W. B. YEATS 19

Sailing to Byzantium W. B. YEATS 21

Among School Children W. B. YEATS 23

To the Fallen Irish Soldiers LORD DUNSANY 26

The Planter's Daughter AUSTIN CLARKE 28

Coole Park, 1929 W. B. YEATS 29

Connolly LIAM MACGABHANN 31

In Memory of Eva Gore-Booth and
   Con Markiewicz W. B. YEATS 33

Inniskeen Road: July Evening PATRICK KAVANAGH 35

The Circus Animals' Desertion W. B. YEATS 36

Dublin LOUIS MACNEICE 38

An Irish Lake W. R. RODGERS 41

Day Ashore   PADRAIC FALLON   43

A Dubliner   BLANAID SALKELD   44

Boy Bathing   DENIS DEVLIN   46

After Five O'Clock   DENIS DEVLIN   47

Spraying the Potatoes   PATRICK KAVANAGH   48

Dublin Made Me   DONAGH MACDONAGH   50

Stony Grey Soil   PATRICK KAVANAGH   52

A Christmas Childhood   PATRICK KAVANAGH   54

First Corncrake   JOHN HEWITT   57

Jackeen ag Caoineadh na mBlascaod   BREANDÁN Ó
    BEACHÁIN 59

A Jackeen Keens for the Blasket   SEÁN HEWITT
    (trans.)   60

The Envy of Poor Lovers   AUSTIN CLARKE   61

O, Come to the Land   PATRICK MACDONOGH   62

Shancoduff   PATRICK KAVANAGH   65

In Memory of My Mother   PATRICK KAVANAGH   66

Kerr's Ass   PATRICK KAVANAGH   68

Epic   PATRICK KAVANAGH   69

Unmarried Mothers   AUSTIN CLARKE   70

Fishguard to Rosslare   CECIL DAY LEWIS   71

Churning Day   SEAMUS HEANEY   72

Inis Oírr   DEREK MAHON   74

Casement's Funeral   RICHARD MURPHY   75

'I saw magic on a green country road –'   MICHAEL
    HARTNETT   77

A Warning to Conquerors   DONAGH MACDONAGH   78

Thatcher   SEAMUS HEANEY   79

Famine Village   RICHARD RYAN   80

The Northern Ireland Question   DESMOND EGAN   81

The Siege of Mullingar   JOHN MONTAGUE   82

Ireland 1972 PAUL DURCAN 84

Death of an Irishwoman MICHAEL HARTNETT 85

Windharp JOHN MONTAGUE 86

Green Beer JAMES J. MCAULEY 87

Old Roads EILÉAN NÍ CHUILLEANÁIN 89

Orange Drums, Tyrone, 1966 SEAMUS HEANEY 90

A Disused Shed in Co. Wexford DEREK MAHON 91

Making Love Outside Áras an Uachtaráin PAUL DURCAN 94

State Funeral THOMAS MCCARTHY 95

A Small Town in Ireland FRANK ORMSBY 97

Casualty SEAMUS HEANEY 98

The Civil Servant MICHAEL LONGLEY 103

Ireland PAUL MULDOON 104

Anseo PAUL MULDOON 105

A Garage in Co. Cork DEREK MAHON 107

Ireland HARRY CLIFTON 110

Facts of Life, Ballymoney EAMON GRENNAN 112

The Death of Irish AIDAN MATHEWS 114

From *Inchicore Haiku*, 25, 37, 55, 82 MICHAEL
    HARTNETT 115

Kinsale DEREK MAHON 116

Holy Well SEÁN DUNNE 117

The Cabinet Table PAUL DURCAN 118

Enemy Encounter PADRAIC FIACC 119

The Emigrant Irish EAVAN BOLAND 120

Belfast Confetti CIARAN CARSON 121

Munster Final BERNARD O'DONOGHUE 122

'When all the others were away at Mass' SEAMUS
    HEANEY 124

Assembling the Parts MICHAEL COADY 125

Ceist na Teangan NUALA NÍ DHOMHNAILL 127

The Language Issue   PAUL MULDOON (trans.)   128

Beara Peninsula   EITHNE STRONG   129

The People I Grew Up with Were Afraid   MICHAEL
   GORMAN   130

Eily Kilbride   BRENDAN KENNELLY   132

The Ice-Cream Man   MICHAEL LONGLEY   133

The Great Blasket Island   JULIE O'CALLAGHAN   134

The Statue of the Virgin at Granard Speaks   PAULA
   MEEHAN   135

A Nun Takes the Veil   BERNARD O'DONOGHUE   139

The Eagle   MATTHEW SWEENEY   141

The State of the Nation   PETER FALLON   143

Cealtrach   MARY O'MALLEY   146

The 'Singer'   MEDBH MCGUCKIAN   148

Inauguration Day   PADDY BUSHE   149

St Mary's Hall   FRANK MCGUINNESS   150

That Summer   EILÉAN NÍ CHUILLEANÁIN   151

Ceasefire   MICHAEL LONGLEY   153

Rural Electrification 1956   MAURICE RIORDAN   155

The Children of Lir   GREG DELANTY   156

Let's Hope   PEARSE HUTCHINSON   157

Postscript   SEAMUS HEANEY   159

St Kevin and the Blackbird   SEAMUS HEANEY   160

Europa Hotel   SINÉAD MORRISSEY   162

Kilmalkedar Church, County Kerry   KERRY HARDIE   163

Testing the Green   SIOBHÁN CAMPBELL   165

Begin   BRENDAN KENNELLY   166

Unlegendary Heroes   MARY O'DONNELL   168

The Flora of County Armagh   SEAN LYSAGHT   171

They That Wash on Thursday   PAUL MULDOON   173

In Donegal   CATHAL MCCABE   175

Ireland: 1967 DERMOT BOLGER 176

Bridge Street LUCY BRENNAN 177

Seatown CONOR O'CALLAGHAN 178

BSE DAVID WHEATLEY 180

July Twelfth MACDARA WOODS 181

Break COLETTE BRYCE 184

Literacy Class, South Inner City PAULA MEEHAN 185

A Prayer MICHAEL LONGLEY 187

Sunday, 16 August 1998 DERMOT HEALY 188

Nineteen Eighty-Four CAITRÍONA O'REILLY 190

Quarantine EAVAN BOLAND 192

Good Friday FRANCIS HARVEY 194

Passing the Royal Hotel, Tipperary Town PATRICK
    MORAN 195

World Music VONA GROARKE 196

The Happiest Day of His Mother's Life VINCENT
    WOODS 198

The Light of Other Days DENNIS O'DRISCOLL 199

This Afternoon JOHN O'DONNELL 202

Ceilidh MICHAEL LONGLEY 204

Catholic Mothers' Monologue MARTINA EVANS 205

Progress ALAN GILLIS 208

Post No Bills CELIA DE FRÉINE 209

1981 COLETTE BRYCE 210

Gethsemene Day DOROTHY MOLLOY 211

A Winter Solstice PETER FALLON 212

Conversation NICK LAIRD 214

Sailing to Byzantium with Mr Yeats MARY ROSE
    CALLAN 215

Muslin PATRICK DEELEY 216

Old Testament Times MARY BRANLEY 217

xii   Munster Football Final 1924   GABRIEL FITZMAURICE   220

PPS   PETER SIRR   221

Female Figure   SUSAN CONNOLLY   223

Death of a Field   PAULA MEEHAN   225

The Final, Galway v. Kerry   GERARD HANBERRY   227

The Irish Poem Is   IGGY MCGOVERN   229

Running with the Immortals   THEO DORGAN   231

Immram: Inis Meáin   LOUISE C. CALLAGHAN   233

Donnelly's Hollow   PAT GALVIN   234

Directive Ireland 2000–2010   GRACE WELLS   237

Made in Ireland   JOE KANE   239

Aerialist   JOHN MCAULIFFE   241

Little Skellig   MOYA CANNON   244

Ireland Is Changing Mother   RITA ANN HIGGINS   246

Ghost Estate   WILLIAM WALL   248

Shrines   MOYA CANNON   250

Indictment   SARAH CLANCY   252

The Moon, the Stars   JOHN F. DEANE   254

The Impact   LEEANNE QUINN   255

Skinny Dipping   JEAN O'BRIEN   257

Slievemore Cemetery Headstones   PAUL DURCAN   258

The First Story   GREG DELANTY   259

Church   JOHN MACKENNA   260

When the Dust Settles   CATHERINE PHIL MACCARTHY   261

The Spire   PAT BORAN   262

Letting Go   VIVIENNE MCKECHNIE   264

Lighthouse   SINÉAD MORRISSEY   266

Shelter from the Storms   TONY CURTIS   267

Hearing Mass   LEANNE O'SULLIVAN   269

St Patrick's Day Address, 1920   TARA BERGIN   270

Death and the Post Office   MARTIN DYAR   271

The Group Scheme   MARTIN DYAR   274   xiii

Homage to Omey   JOAN MCBREEN   276

Porn   ANNE HAVERTY   277

Tans   TOM FRENCH   279

A Spiritual People   ANTHONY CRONIN   280

An Education in Silence   JESSICA TRAYNOR   283

The Angel of History   THEO DORGAN   284

The Eucharistic Congress 2012   NOEL MONAHAN   286

Promises, Promises   GERALD DAWE   287

Waking   DOIREANN NÍ GHRÍOFA   288

Fields   JOHN FITZGERALD   289

St Patrick's Day   ENDA WYLEY   290

Neutral Ireland   GERARD SMYTH   291

Famine Cottages   SARA BERKELEY   292

The Countermanding Order, 1916   MOYA CANNON   294

Acknowledgements   297

Index of Poets   311

Index of Titles   315

Introduction

Nothing is ever lost that makes its way into poetry.

– Paula Meehan

Ireland is known for its poetry, and Ireland is known through its poems and poets. In *An Apology for Poetry*, first published in 1595, the English poet and soldier Sir Philip Sidney claimed that 'In our neighbour country Ireland where true learning goes very bare, yet are their poets held in a devout reverence.' Whether or not Sidney's first observation was or remains accurate, Ireland certainly still respects and values its poets. They remake the language; they tell the truth as they see it; they challenge us and open us up to the world; they rearrange how we view it.

The poems in this anthology are not only the work of Irish authors; they are poems of Ireland. They speak in various ways of the country's people and beliefs, its landscape, its passions and politics, and the extraordinary changes that have occurred over the past hundred years. They are arranged chronologically, by year of first publication in volume form, with the exception of three poems – Patrick Pearse's 'The Wayfarer', W. B. Yeats's 'Easter 1916' and Michael Longley's 'Ceasefire' – that are inextricably linked to events in the year in which they were composed. An effort has been made to represent the full span of the century, but some periods are naturally richer than others; and the dating policy means, for example, that Patrick Kavanagh's glorious output of the 1950s – otherwise not a very strong decade for Irish poetry – is assigned to 1960, when it appeared in his collection *Come Dance with Kitty Stobling,* his first in thirteen years. (Another poet, Thomas Kinsella, who published his first great work in the 1950s, unfortunately declined to be anthologized here.) And of course, regardless of date of composition or publication, many poems here speak to the past; and so, while Maurice Riordan's 'Rural Electrification 1956', for example, was published in 1995, it contributes to this book's portrait of mid-century Ireland.

Yeats, in Seamus Heaney's words, 'put Ireland among the nations of the world. He is there in the way a mountain range rises above a plain.' There are a number of great poets represented in this anthology, but I am also pleased to include less established poets and younger voices. Young Irish poets, said Kate O'Brien, 'need to bring their own wild news to life'. I hope that the poems included here speak to and answer one another, and tell the 'wild news' of Ireland in a distinctive way.

Niall MacMonagle

Pearse, aged thirty-six, wrote 'The Wayfarer' in the knowledge that he was to face a firing squad the following morning, having been found guilty of treason for his part in the Easter Rising. Though the poem paints a picture of a heaven on earth – evening sunshine, an unspoilt natural world, innocent children at play – the sad note struck in the opening line is heard again, and the final line, with its falling rhythm, is a one-word lonely one. 'It may be sampler poetry,' says the novelist Eugene McCabe, 'but because of the context it is overwhelming.' On 3 May 1916, at 3.30 a.m., Pearse was shot dead in the Stonebreakers' Yard of Kilmainham Gaol.

The Wayfarer

The beauty of the world hath made me sad,
This beauty that will pass;
Sometimes my heart hath shaken with great joy
To see a leaping squirrel in a tree,
Or a red lady-bird upon a stalk,
Or little rabbits in a field at evening,
Lit by a slanting sun,
Or some green hill where shadows drifted by
Some quiet hill where mountainy man hath sown
And soon would reap; near to the gate of Heaven;
Or children with bare feet upon the sands
Of some ebbed sea, or playing on the streets
Of little towns in Connacht,
Things young and happy.
And then my heart hath told me:
These will pass,

Will pass and change, will die and be no more,
Things bright and green, things young and happy;
And I have gone upon my way
Sorrowful.

This poem is one soldier's lament for a fellow soldier, one Irish poet's lament for a fellow Irish poet. Francis Ledwidge, born into great poverty, worked as a farm boy, a labourer and a miner before enlisting in the British Army in 1914. He fought in the Great War 'neither for a principle nor a people nor a law, but for the fields along the Boyne, for the birds and the blue sky over them'. Both poets were talented. Francis Ledwidge had a promising career as a writer; James Stephens said of him that 'His promise is, I think, greater than that of any young poet now writing.' Yeats, in his poem 'Easter 1916', says of MacDonagh that he 'might have won fame in the end,/So sensitive his nature seemed,/So daring and sweet his thought.' Ledwidge saw action at Gallipoli and in the Balkans before being killed by a shell on 31 July 1917 near Ypres. In his elegy for Ledwidge, Seamus Heaney laments 'the twilit note your flute should sound'.

Lament for Thomas MacDonagh

He shall not hear the bittern cry
In the wild sky, where he is lain,
Nor voices of the sweeter birds
Above the wailing of the rain.

Nor shall he know when loud March blows
Thro' slanting snows her fanfare shrill,
Blowing to flame the golden cup
Of many an upset daffodil.

But when the Dark Cow leaves the moor,
And pastures poor with greedy weeds,
Perhaps he'll hear her low at morn
Lifting her horn in pleasant meads.

W. B. Yeats, 1916

The events of Easter Monday 1916 took Yeats by surprise. Three years earlier he had written that 'Romantic Ireland's dead and gone'; now he admits that he misjudged the men and women who had fought for a cause that they passionately believed in. The recurring, varying couplet, according to Micheál Mac Liammóir and Eavan Boland in their book *W. B. Yeats and His World*, 'with its insistent, irregular, beaten-out rhythm, like that of mournful bells, has become to Irish ears as familiar as a nightly prayer'. This poem's four stanzas, each containing sixteen or twenty-four lines, memorializes the day, the month and the year – 24.4.16 – of the Rising.

Easter 1916

I have met them at close of day
Coming with vivid faces
From counter or desk among grey
Eighteenth-century houses.
I have passed with a nod of the head
Or polite meaningless words,
Or have lingered awhile and said
Polite meaningless words,
And thought before I had done
Of a mocking tale or a gibe
To please a companion
Around the fire at the club,
Being certain that they and I
But lived where motley is worn:
All changed, changed utterly:
A terrible beauty is born.

That woman's days were spent
In ignorant good-will,
Her nights in argument
Until her voice grew shrill.
What voice more sweet than hers
When, young and beautiful,
She rode to harriers?
This man had kept a school
And rode our wingèd horse;
This other his helper and friend
Was coming into his force;
He might have won fame in the end,
So sensitive his nature seemed,
So daring and sweet his thought.
This other man I had dreamed
A drunken, vainglorious lout.
He had done most bitter wrong
To some who are near my heart,
Yet I number him in the song;
He, too, has resigned his part
In the casual comedy;
He, too, has been changed in his turn,
Transformed utterly:
A terrible beauty is born.

Hearts with one purpose alone
Through summer and winter seem
Enchanted to a stone
To trouble the living stream.
The horse that comes from the road,

The rider, the birds that range
From cloud to tumbling cloud,
Minute by minute they change;
A shadow of cloud on the stream
Changes minute by minute;
A horse-hoof slides on the brim,
And a horse plashes within it;
The long-legged moor-hens dive,
And hens to moor-cocks call;
Minute by minute they live:
The stone's in the midst of all.

Too long a sacrifice
Can make a stone of the heart.
O when may it suffice?
That is Heaven's part, our part
To murmur name upon name,
As a mother names her child
When sleep at last has come
On limbs that had run wild.
What is it but nightfall?
No, no, not night but death;
Was it needless death after all?
For England may keep faith
For all that is done and said.
We know their dream; enough
To know they dreamed and are dead;
And what if excess of love
Bewildered them till they died?
I write it out in a verse –

MacDonagh and MacBride
And Connolly and Pearse
Now and in time to be,
Wherever green is worn,
Are changed, changed utterly:
A terrible beauty is born.

25 September 1916

Tom Kettle, whom President Michael D. Higgins called 'an Irish patriot, a British soldier and a true European' in his speech at Windsor Castle in April 2014, wrote this sonnet 'in the field, before Guillemont, Somme, 4 September 1916'. He was born in Dublin in 1880, educated at Clongowes and UCD, studied law and was called to the Bar. Kettle joined the Irish Volunteers and their fight for Irish independence in 1913. When Britain declared war on Germany, he sided with John Redmond, Nationalist MP, whose goal was Home Rule and who, by June 1914, had control of the Volunteers. Redmond feared the Irish Volunteers might hinder the enactment of Home Rule and encouraged them to join the British Army. Kettle enlisted and sailed for France on 14 July 1916. He was killed in action on 9 September. There is no known grave. The erection of a memorial bust in St Stephen's Green was delayed until 1937, owing to a dispute between Kettle's family and friends, who insisted that the last three lines of this poem be engraved on the plinth, and the OPW, which opposed the inscription. In the end, the bust – with the lines included – was unveiled without official ceremony.

To My Daughter Betty, The Gift of God

In wiser days, my darling rosebud, blown
To beauty proud as was your mother's prime,
In that desired, delayed, incredible time,
You'll ask why I abandoned you, my own,
And the dear heart that was your baby throne,
To dice with death. And, oh! they'll give you rhyme
And reason: some will call the thing sublime,
And some decry it in a knowing tone.

So here, while the mad guns curse overhead,
And tired men sigh, with mud for couch and floor,
Know that we fools, now with the foolish dead,
Died not for flag, nor King, nor Emperor,
But for a dream, born in a herdsman's shed,
And for the secret Scripture of the poor.

Katharine Tynan, 1916

Over 200,000 Irishmen fought in the First World War and tens of thousands never came home. Katharine Tynan, born at Whitehall dairy farm in Clondalkin, west Dublin, uses the simple domestic image of boys returning home from school to highlight the sadness created by the absence of the young men who had gone to fight in the war.

The Long Vacation

This is the time the boys come home from school,
  Filling the house with gay and happy noise,
Never at rest from morn till evening cool –
  All the roads of the world bring home the boys.

This is the time – but still they are not come;
  The mothers stand in the doorway listening long;
Long, long they shall wait ere the boys come home.
  Where do they tarry, the dear, the light-heart throng?

Their feet are heavy as lead and deep their rest.
  The mothers watch the road till set of sun;
But nevermore the birds fly back to the nest.
  The roads of the world run Heavenward every one.

Eva Gore-Booth – who is today best remembered as the 'gazelle' in Yeats's poem 'In Memory of Eva Gore-Booth and Con Markiewicz' – was a serious poet in her own right. Though born into privilege and wealth at Lissadell, she had little interest in fashionable society. She was, according to her partner Esther Roper, 'haunted by the suffering of the world' and had 'a curious feeling of responsibility for its inequalities and injustices'. In Manchester, Gore-Booth worked for the political and economic enfranchisement of women. This poem is addressed to her sister Constance, who was an officer of the Citizen Army in the Easter Rising; a sentence of death was commuted to life imprisonment on account of her sex. A month after Eva Gore-Booth died, in 1926, her elder sister wrote: 'Her human presence was so beautiful and wonderful, but with her the spirit dominated every bit of her and her body was just the human instrument it shone through.'

Comrades

The peaceful night that round me flows,
Breaks through your iron prison doors,
Free through the world your spirit goes,
Forbidden hands are clasping yours.

The wind is our confederate,
The night has left her doors ajar,
We meet beyond earth's barrèd gate,
Where all the world's wild Rebels are.

Fifteen rebels were executed in May 1916 for their part in the Easter Rising. Shortly after the last of these executions, Roger Casement was tried in London for high treason. Casement, who had been in Germany seeking to arrange shipments of arms to assist the Rising, travelled to Ireland in a German submarine, and was captured shortly after landing in County Kerry, three days before Easter Monday. Dora Sigerson Shorter imagines the executed fifteen waiting for Casement and being joined by him as he comes through the gate of Pentonville Prison. In figuring Casement as 'their Captain', the poem overstates Casement's influence among the men who led the Rising, but reflects the high regard in which he was held by separatists.

Sixteen Dead Men

Hark! In the still night. Who goes there?
   'Fifteen dead men.' Why do they wait?
'Hasten, comrade, death is so fair.'
   Now comes their Captain through the dim gate.

Sixteen dead men! What on their sword?
   'A nation's honour proud do they bear.'
What on their bent heads? *'God's holy word;*
   All of their nation's heart blended in prayer.'

Sixteen dead men! What makes their shroud?
   'All of their nation's love wraps them around.'
Where do their bodies lie, brave and so proud?
   'Under the gallows-tree in prison ground.'

Sixteen dead men! Where do they go?
  'To join their regiment, where Sarsfield leads;
Wolfe Tone and Emmet, too, well do they know:
  There shall they bivouac, telling great deeds.'

Sixteen dead men! Shall they return?
  'Yea, they shall come again, breath of our breath
They on our nation's hearth made old fires burn,
  Guard her unconquered soul, strong in their death.'

Thomas MacGreevy, 1921

On 14 March 1921, during the War of Independence, six IRA men – Thomas Bryan (an electrician and recently married), Patrick Doyle (carpenter and father of four), Frank Flood (a student at UCD), Paddy Moran (who had fought under Thomas MacDonagh in 1916), Bernard Ryan (an apprentice tailor and breadwinner who lived with his widowed mother) and Thomas Whelan (who sang a song for his mother, 'The Shawl of Galway Grey', the night before he was executed) – were convicted of treason and hanged in Mountjoy Gaol. Almost 20,000 people gathered that morning to pray and sing hymns outside the prison. At six o'clock, at seven and at eight, bells tolled to signal that two men had been hanged on the hour. This poem creates the atmosphere in the men's cells before the hanging and the fervent, prayerful cry of the mainly female crowd. MacGreevy was a young man, a veteran of the Western Front, when he wrote this poem; in later years his poetry would be influenced by modernism, and he became perhaps the most trusted confidant of the young Samuel Beckett.

The Six Who Were Hanged

The sky turns limpid green.
The stars go silver white.
They must be sitting in their cells now –

Unspeaking likely!

Waiting for an attack
With death uncertain
One said little.

For these there is no uncertainty.

The sun will come soon,
All gold.

'Tis you shall have the golden throne –

It will come ere its time.
It will not be time,
Oh, it will not be time,
Not for silver and gold,
Not with green,
Till they all have dropped home,
Till gaol bells all have clanged,
Till all six have been hanged.

And after?
Will it be time?

There are two to be hanged at six o'clock.

Two others at seven,
And the others,
The epilogue two,
At eight.
The sun will have risen
And two will be hanging
In green, white and gold,
In a premature Easter.

The white-faced stars are silent,
Silent the pale sky;
Up on his iron car
The small conqueror's robot
Sits quiet.
But *Hail Mary! Hail Mary!*
They say it and say it,
These hundreds of lamenting women and girls
Holding Crucified Christs.

Daughters of Jerusalem . . .

Perhaps women have Easters.

There are very few men.
Why am I here?

At the hour of our death
At this hour of youth's death,
Hail Mary! Hail Mary!
Now young bodies swing up
Then
Young souls
Slip after the stars.
Hail Mary! Hail Mary!

Alas! I am not their Saint John –

Tired of sorrow,
My sorrow, their sorrow, all sorrow,

I go from the hanged,
From the women,
I go from the hanging;
Scarcely moved by the thought of the two to
   be hanged
I go from the epilogue.

Morning Star, Pray for us!

What, these seven hundred years
Has Ireland had to do
With the morning star?

And still, I too say,
Pray for us.

Mountjoy, March 1921

Austin Clarke, 1925

In *Mother Ireland*, Edna O'Brien observes that 'Ireland has always been a woman, a womb, a cave, a cow, a Rosaleen, a sow, a bride, a harlot, and, of course, the gaunt Hag of Beare.' Here, the heifer is an image for Ireland at a time when the country was beginning to forge a new identity. Clarke wrote that the poem was composed 'during a period when our national idealism suffered eclipse. The Heifer or Silk of the Kine is a secret name used by the Jacobite poets for Ireland.'

The Lost Heifer

When the black herds of the rain were grazing
In the gap of the pure cold wind
And the watery hazes of the hazel
Brought her into my mind,
I thought of the last honey by the water
That no hive can find.

Brightness was drenching through the branches
When she wandered again,
Turning the silver out of dark grasses
Where the skylark had lain,
And her voice coming softly over the meadow
Was the mist becoming rain.

Yeats began working on his long poem 'Meditations in Time of Civil War' at Thoor Ballylee in 1922: 'I was in my Galway house during the first months of civil war, the railway bridges blown up and the roads blocked with stones and trees. For the first week there were no newspapers, no reliable news, we did not know who had won nor who had lost, and even after newspapers came, one never knew what was happening on the other side of the hill or of the line of trees. Ford cars passed the house from time to time with coffins standing upon end between the seats, and sometimes at night we heard an explosion, and once by day saw the smoke made by the burning of a great neighbouring house. Men must have lived so through many tumultuous centuries. One felt an overmastering desire not to grow unhappy or embittered, not to lose all sense of the beauty of nature. A stare (our West of Ireland name for a starling) had built in a hole beside my window and I made these verses out of the feeling of the moment . . . Presently a strange thing happened; I began to smell honey in places where honey could not be, at the end of a stone passage or at some windy turn of the road.' Section VI of 'Meditations', titled 'The Stare's Nest by My Window', captures the confusion of this time.

The Stare's Nest by My Window

The bees build in the crevices
Of loosening masonry, and there
The mother birds bring grubs and flies.
My wall is loosening; honey-bees,
Come build in the empty house of the stare.

We are closed in, and the key is turned
On our uncertainty; somewhere
A man is killed, or a house burned,
Yet no clear fact to be discerned:
Come build in the empty house of the stare.

A barricade of stone or of wood;
Some fourteen days of civil war;
Last night they trundled down the road
That dead young soldier in his blood:
Come build in the empty house of the stare.

We had fed the heart on fantasies,
The heart's grown brutal from the fare;
More substance in our enmities
Than in our love; O honey-bees,
Come build in the empty house of the stare.

Yeats said that in this poem, known to generations of Irish school-children, he was 'trying to write about the state of my soul, for it is right for an old man to make his soul'.

Sailing to Byzantium

I

That is no country for old men. The young
In one another's arms, birds in the trees
– Those dying generations – at their song,
The salmon-falls, the mackerel-crowded seas,
Fish, flesh, or fowl, commend all summer long
Whatever is begotten, born, and dies.
Caught in that sensual music all neglect
Monuments of unageing intellect.

II

An aged man is but a paltry thing,
A tattered coat upon a stick, unless
Soul clap its hands and sing, and louder sing
For every tatter in its mortal dress,
Nor is there singing school but studying
Monuments of its own magnificence;
And therefore I have sailed the seas and come
To the holy city of Byzantium.

III

O sages standing in God's holy fire
As in the gold mosaic of a wall,
Come from the holy fire, perne in a gyre,
And be the singing-masters of my soul.
Consume my heart away; sick with desire
And fastened to a dying animal
It knows not what it is; and gather me
Into the artifice of eternity.

IV

Once out of nature I shall never take
My bodily form from any natural thing,
But such a form as Grecian goldsmiths make
Of hammered gold and gold enamelling
To keep a drowsy Emperor awake;
Or set upon a golden bough to sing
To lords and ladies of Byzantium
Of what is past, or passing, or to come.

Seamus Heaney likened reading Yeats to feeling 'at times a transmission of dangerous force such as I felt as a child, standing alone in fields close to the tremble of electric poles, under the sizzle of power lines'. In 'Sailing to Byzantium', Yeats's chosen ideal is a golden bird upon a golden bough. In 'Among School Children', a tree and a dancer represent harmony, perfection and immortality. This poem, a meditation on life's journey from childhood to old age, was prompted by a visit Yeats had made to St Otteran's School, Waterford, in February 1926.

Among School Children

I

I walk through the long schoolroom questioning;
A kind old nun in a white hood replies;
The children learn to cipher and to sing,
To study reading-books and histories
To cut and sew, be neat in everything
In the best modern way – the children's eyes
In momentary wonder stare upon
A sixty-year-old smiling public man.

II

I dream of a Ledaean body, bent
Above a sinking fire, a tale that she
Told of a harsh reproof, or trivial event
That changed some childish day to tragedy –
Told, and it seemed that our two natures blent
Into a sphere from youthful sympathy,
Or else, to alter Plato's parable,
Into the yolk and white of the one shell.

III

And thinking of that fit of grief or rage
I look upon one child or t'other there
And wonder if she stood so at that age –
For even daughters of the swan can share
Something of every paddler's heritage –
And had that colour upon cheek or hair,
And thereupon my heart is driven wild:
She stands before me as a living child.

IV

Her present image floats into the mind –
Did Quattrocento finger fashion it
Hollow of cheek as though it drank the wind
And took a mess of shadows for its meat?
And I though never of Ledaean kind
Had pretty plumage once – enough of that,
Better to smile on all that smile, and show
There is a comfortable kind of old scarecrow.

V

What youthful mother, a shape upon her lap
Honey of generation had betrayed,
And that must sleep, shriek, struggle to escape
As recollection or the drug decide,
Would think her son, did she but see that shape
With sixty or more winters on its head,
A compensation for the pang of his birth,
Or the uncertainty of his setting forth?

VI

Plato thought nature but a spume that plays
Upon a ghostly paradigm of things;
Solider Aristotle played the taws
Upon the bottom of a king of kings;
World-famous golden-thighed Pythagoras
Fingered upon a fiddle-stick or strings
What a star sang and careless Muses heard:
Old clothes upon old sticks to scare a bird.

VII

Both nuns and mothers worship images,
But those the candles light are not as those
That animate a mother's reveries,
But keep a marble or a bronze repose.
And yet they too break hearts – O Presences
That passion, piety or affection knows,
And that all heavenly glory symbolise –
O self-born mockers of man's enterprise;

VIII

Labour is blossoming or dancing where
The body is not bruised to pleasure soul,
Nor beauty born out of its own despair,
Nor blear-eyed wisdom out of midnight oil.
O chestnut-tree, great-rooted blossomer,
Are you the leaf, the blossom or the bole?
O body swayed to music, O brightening glance,
How can we know the dancer from the dance?

Edward John Moreton Drax Plunkett, Baron of Dunsany, London born, inherited the family title and estate near Tara, in County Meath. He was an officer in the Coldstream Guards during the Boer War, and in the Royal Inniskilling Fusiliers during the First World War. While on leave in Dublin in April 1916, he was shot in the face when he drove into Dublin to support the British forces in suppressing the Easter Rising. This poem remembers those Irish who fought on the Continent during the war, who would not be officially acknowledged by the Irish state for decades. A war memorial was planned for Merrion Square but never built; eventually a memorial park was created at Islandbridge, and opened thirty years after the end of the war. When Queen Elizabeth II visited Ireland in 2011 she and President Mary McAleese visited Islandbridge and laid wreaths. In 2008 President McAleese unveiled a national memorial, in Merrion Square, to members of the Defence Forces who died in the service of the state.

To the Fallen Irish Soldiers

Since they have grudged you space in Merrion Square,
    And any monument of stone or brass,
    And you yourselves are powerless, alas,
And your own countrymen seem not to care;
Let then these words of mine drift down the air,
    Lest the world think that it has come to pass
    That *all* in Ireland treat as common grass
The soil that wraps her heroes slumbering there.

Sleep on, forgot a few more years, and then
    The ages, that I prophesy, shall see

Due honours paid to you by juster men,
    You standing foremost in our history,
Your story filling all our land with wonder,
Your names, and regiments' names, like distant thunder.

Ireland is sometimes seen as a nation of begrudgers; but Clarke's poem recognizes a generous, admiring quality. The effect of the planter's daughter on her neighbours is figured in very Irish terms: drink, talk and religion. The poem illustrates what Clarke identified as his main theme: 'the drama of racial consciousness'.

The Planter's Daughter

When night stirred at sea
And the fire brought a crowd in,
They say that her beauty
Was music in mouth
And few in the candlelight
Thought her too proud,
For the house of the planter
Is known by the trees.

Men that had seen her
Drank deep and were silent,
The women were speaking
Wherever she went –
As a bell that is rung
Or a wonder told shyly,
And O she was the Sunday
In every week.

The thousand-acre Coole Park belonged to the Gregory family since the 1760s and, in the early twentieth century, Lady Gregory hosted writers and intellectuals whose energies and efforts created a literary revival that helped to forge a nation's identity. Lady Gregory sold the house to the state in 1927, but retained residency and died there in 1932. It was demolished in 1941.

Coole Park, 1929

I meditate upon a swallow's flight,
Upon an aged woman and her house,
A sycamore and lime-tree lost in night
Although that western cloud is luminous,
Great works constructed there in nature's spite
For scholars and for poets after us,
Thoughts long knitted into a single thought,
A dance-like glory that those walls begot.

There Hyde before he had beaten into prose
That noble blade the Muses buckled on,
There one that ruffled in a manly pose
For all his timid heart, there that slow man,
That meditative man, John Synge, and those
Impetuous men, Shawe-Taylor and Hugh Lane,
Found pride established in humility,
A scene well set and excellent company.

They came like swallows and like swallows went,
And yet a woman's powerful character
Could keep a swallow to its first intent;
And half a dozen in formation there,
That seemed to whirl upon a compass-point,
Found certainty upon the dreaming air,
The intellectual sweetness of those lines
That cut through time or cross it withershins.

Here, traveller, scholar, poet, take your stand
When all those rooms and passages are gone,
When nettles wave upon a shapeless mound
And saplings root among the broken stone,
And dedicate – eyes bent upon the ground,
Back turned upon the brightness of the sun
And all the sensuality of the shade –
A moment's memory to that laurelled head.

The speaker – a British soldier, as MacGabhann said in his own note on the poem – remembers with sorrow, regret and unease his part in the execution of James Connolly in Kilmainham Gaol on 12 May 1916. Connolly had been badly wounded during the Easter Rising, and thus could not stand before the firing squad; instead he was strapped to a chair. Michael Collins said of him: 'Connolly I'd follow into Hell. Pearse I'd have to think about.'

Connolly

The man was all shot through that came today
Into the barrack square;
A soldier I – I am not proud to say
We killed him there;
They brought him from the prison hospital;
To see him in that chair
I thought his smile would far more quickly call
A man to prayer.

Maybe we cannot understand this thing
That makes these rebels die;
And yet all things love freedom – and the Spring
Clear in the sky;
I think I would not do this deed again
For all that I hold by;
Gaze down my rifle at his breast – but then
A soldier I.

They say that he was kindly – different too,
Apart from all the rest;
A lover of the poor; and all shot through,
His wounds ill drest,
He came before us, faced us like a man,
He knew a deeper pain
Than blows or bullets – ere the world began;
Died he in vain?

Ready – present; And he just smiling – God!
I felt my rifle shake
His wounds were opened out and round that chair
Was one red lake;
I swear his lips said 'Fire!' when all was still
Before my rifle spat
That cursed lead – and I was picked to kill
A man like that!

In a letter to Eva Gore-Booth, dated 23 July 1916, Yeats wrote, 'Your sister & yourself, two beautiful figures among the great trees of Lissadell, are among the dear memories of my youth.' The poem he wrote after they died dwells on the enemy that is time, the sorrows that change and disappointment bring, and the fading of Ireland's Protestant Ascendancy.

In Memory of Eva Gore-Booth and Con Markiewicz

I

The light of evening, Lissadell,
Great windows open to the south,
Two girls in silk kimonos, both
Beautiful, one a gazelle.
But a raving autumn shears
Blossom from the summer's wreath;
The older is condemned to death,
Pardoned, drags out lonely years
Conspiring among the ignorant.
I know not what the younger dreams –
Some vague Utopia – and she seems,
When withered old and skeleton-gaunt,
An image of such politics.
Many a time I think to seek
One or the other out and speak
Of that old Georgian mansion, mix
Pictures of the mind, recall
That table and the talk of youth,
Two girls in silk kimonos, both
Beautiful, one a gazelle.

34

II

Dear shadows, now you know it all,
All the folly of a fight
With a common wrong or right.
The innocent and the beautiful
Have no enemy but time;
Arise and bid me strike a match
And strike another till time catch;
Should the conflagration climb,
Run till all the sages know.
We the great gazebo built,
They convicted us of guilt;
Bid me strike a match and blow.

In 1962 Patrick Kavanagh said that 'A poet is never one of the people. He is detached, remote, and the life of small-time dances and talk about football would not be for him. He might take part but he could not belong.' This poem from Kavanagh's first collection is perhaps his most eloquent articulation of this idea.

Inniskeen Road: July Evening

The bicycles go by in twos and threes –
There's a dance in Billy Brennan's barn tonight,
And there's the half-talk code of mysteries
And the wink-and-elbow language of delight.
Half-past eight and there is not a spot
Upon a mile of road, no shadow thrown
That might turn out a man or woman, not
A footfall tapping secrecies of stone.

I have what every poet hates in spite
Of all the solemn talk of contemplation.
Oh, Alexander Selkirk knew the plight
Of being king and government and nation.
A road, a mile of kingdom, I am king
Of banks and stones and every blooming thing.

In this poem, among the last he would ever write, Yeats – man and artist – takes stock. He revisits the themes that preoccupied him, the Irish myths and heroes that he brought to the stage, his passion for Maud Gonne, his heartbreak and disappointment. The speaker here calls himself 'a broken man', and by the closing stanza Yeats recognizes that all great art has its origin in the ordinary.

The Circus Animals' Desertion

I

I sought a theme and sought for it in vain,
I sought it daily for six weeks or so.
Maybe at last, being but a broken man,
I must be satisfied with my heart, although
Winter and summer till old age began
My circus animals were all on show,
Those stilted boys, that burnished chariot,
Lion and woman and the Lord knows what.

II

What can I but enumerate old themes?
First that sea-rider Oisin led by the nose
Through three enchanted islands, allegorical dreams,
Vain gaiety, vain battle, vain repose,
Themes of the embittered heart, or so it seems,
That might adorn old songs or courtly shows;
But what cared I that set him on to ride,
I, starved for the bosom of his faery bride?

And then a counter-truth filled out its play,
The Countess Cathleen was the name I gave it;
She, pity-crazed, had given her soul away,
But masterful Heaven had intervened to save it.
I thought my dear must her own soul destroy,
So did fanaticism and hate enslave it,
And this brought forth a dream and soon enough
This dream itself had all my thought and love.

And when the Fool and Blind Man stole the bread
Cuchulain fought the ungovernable sea;
Heart-mysteries there, and yet when all is said
It was the dream itself enchanted me:
Character isolated by a deed
To engross the present and dominate memory.
Players and painted stage took all my love,
And not those things that they were emblems of.

III

Those masterful images because complete
Grew in pure mind, but out of what began?
A mound of refuse or the sweepings of a street,
Old kettles, old bottles, and a broken can,
Old iron, old bones, old rags, that raving slut
Who keeps the till. Now that my ladder's gone,
I must lie down where all the ladders start,
In the foul rag-and-bone shop of the heart.

Born in Belfast, brought up in Carrickfergus, educated in England, MacNeice, 'the rector's son, born to the anglican order,/Banned for ever from the candles of the Irish poor', was nonetheless drawn to Dublin: 'she holds my mind'. The statues of O'Connell, Grattan and Moore stand for politics, poetry and music from the eighteenth and nineteenth centuries; the monument to Admiral Nelson reminds us that Dublin, with its dilapidated Georgian houses, was once the second city of the British Empire. This poem is from a sequence originally titled 'The Coming of War', later renamed 'The Closing Album'.

Dublin

Grey brick upon brick,
Declamatory bronze
On sombre pedestals –
O'Connell, Grattan, Moore –
And the brewery tugs and the swans
On the balustraded stream
And the bare bones of a fanlight
Over a hungry door
And the air soft on the cheek
And porter running from the taps
With a head of yellow cream
And Nelson on his pillar
Watching his world collapse.

This was never my town,
I was not born nor bred
Nor schooled here and she will not

Have me alive or dead.
But yet she holds my mind
With her seedy elegance,
With her gentle veils of rain
And all her ghosts that walk
And all that hide behind
Her Georgian façades –
The catcalls and the pain,
The glamour of her squalor,
The bravado of her talk.

The lights jig in the river
With a concertina movement
And the sun comes up in the morning
Like barley-sugar on the water
And the mist on the Wicklow hills
Is close, as close
As the peasantry were to the landlord,
As the Irish to the Anglo-Irish,
As the killer is close one moment
To the man he kills,
Or as the moment itself
Is close to the next moment.

She is not an Irish town
And she is not English,
Historic with guns and vermin
And the cold renown
Of a fragment of Church Latin,
Of an oratorical phrase.

But oh the days are soft,
Soft enough to forget
The lesson better learnt,
The bullet on the wet
Streets, the crooked deal,
The steel behind the laugh,
The Four Courts burnt.

Fort of the Dane,
Garrison of the Saxon,
Augustan capital
Of a Gaelic nation,
Appropriating all
The alien brought,
You give me time for thought
And by a juggler's trick
You poise the toppling hour –
O greyness run to flower,
Grey stone, grey water
And brick upon grey brick.

The natural world, often a repository of inspiration for poets, is here depicted in the sinister shadow of the Second World War. Rodgers, a Presbyterian minister, was based in Loughgall, County Armagh, when he wrote this poem.

An Irish Lake

There in the hard light
Dark birds, pink-footed, dab and pick
Among the addery roots and marrowy stones,
And the blown waves blink and hiccup at the lake's
Lip. A late bee blares and drones on inland
Into a cone-point of silence, and I
Lying at the rhododendron's foot
Look through five fingers' grille at the lake
Shaking, at the bare and backward plain, and
The running and bending hills that carry
Like a conveyer belt the bright snail-line
Of clouds along the sky all day unendingly.

There, far from the slack noose of rumour
That tightens into choking fact, I relax,
And sounds and sights and scents sail slowly by.
But suddenly, like delicate and tilted italics,
The up-standing birds stretch urgently away
Into the sky as suddenly grown grey.
Night rounds on Europe now. And I must go.
Before its hostile faces peer and pour

Over the mind's rim enveloping me,
And my so-frightened thoughts dart here and there
Like trout among their grim stony gazes.

Eavan Boland says that Padraic Fallon's poetry is 'talky and musical, both at once'. This poem, one of an eight-poem sequence called 'Coastal Waters', captures a Sunday mood that is becoming more and more rare.

Day Ashore

Sundays the long boat of the week
Is drawn up, turned keel over on the sand;
Rest, fellows, on the old
Wall, bellying the wind.

Here the sea colour shoals
And the Pole fails to pull. Rest, fellows,
On your rock pillows
And the small seas that sleep in shells.

Tomorrow the heave as earth turns over
Into Monday. Take your ease.
Light the pipe. Sit on forever.
Forget you're cold saltwater to the knees.

Salkeld was born Blanaid ffrench Mullen in Chittagong, and spent her childhood in Ireland. She married an Englishman and lived for a time in Bombay, but returned to Ireland a young widow with her children in 1908. She was active in the nationalist movement, acted on the Abbey stage, and wrote in Irish and English. Every age has its conventions and its pressures to conform. In 'A Dubliner', Salkeld warns against deadening conformity and materialism and celebrates artistic individuality. (Her e e cummings-like unspaced commas have been retained here.)

A Dubliner

Every dead Dubliner here wishes
To be in the mode,or hoard up riches;
Instead of himself laying siege to the deep girl Fame,
He tacks on to her vexed suitors some egregious name.

I admire the scowling infant's savage look,
Crumpling the new attempted copy-book,
For these are fertile tears that wet
His crooked and obscure alphabet.
There must be painters hunger-poor,
Smash down their palettes to the floor,
Who out of hope,still inly burn

To set permanence on a light hand's-turn.
Dry critics hop from hearth to hall;
Old Silence gapes to swallow all.

Echoes,selfless,cold history will blame us –
Nestless,flutterers after the famous.
I cry,and I fly in my own weather,
She said; I am not of their father:
They never clinked two rhyming straws together.

What the Italian philosopher Mario Rossi calls the great interests of man – 'air and light, the joy of having a body, the voluptuousness of looking' – are all celebrated in a poem by one of Ireland's leading modernist poets.

Boy Bathing

On the edge of the springboard
A boy poses, columned light
Poised.
Seagulls' crying wrinkles
The brown parchment cliffs.
His body shines: a knife!
Spread wings, he opens
Plunges
Through the gold glass of sunshine
Smashes
In crumbs of glass the silence.

After time spent training for the priesthood, living in Paris and teaching English in UCD, Devlin entered the Department of Foreign Affairs. The location of the events described in this poem is not clear, but the Irishness of the official seems unmistakable.

After Five O'Clock

A Government official dressed in grey minor
Slipped into a low pub
At the end of the world;
Outside, the rain was falling in millions.

An ancient like a frittered, chalk hill
Monocled the evening paper through a chip of window-pane:
The disgraced words took on dignity.

'Will he tout me for a drink?' feared the Government official
Though the ancient stirred no more than thought in a
    new-dead man.

Patrick Kavanagh, 1947

This is a poem of sounds, sensations and neighbourly conversation. It portrays a style of farming that now belongs to the past. Kavanagh, in a school essay, wrote that 'the lover of nature . . . can see beauty in everything. He can see the finger of God even in a nettle.'

Spraying the Potatoes

The barrels of blue potato-spray
Stood on a headland of July
Beside an orchard wall where roses
Were young girls hanging from the sky.

The flocks of green potato-stalks
Were blossom spread for sudden flight,
The Kerr's Pinks in a frivelled blue,
The Arran Banners wearing white.

And over that potato-field
A lazy veil of woven sun.
Dandelions growing on headlands, showing
Their unloved hearts to everyone.

And I was there with the knapsack sprayer
On the barrel's edge poised. A wasp was floating
Dead on a sunken briar leaf
Over a copper-poisoned ocean.

The axle-roll of a rut-locked cart
Broke the burnt stick of noon in two.
An old man came through a corn-field
Remembering his youth and some Ruth he knew.

He turned my way. 'God further the work.'
He echoed an ancient farming prayer.
I thanked him. He eyed the potato-drills.
He said: 'You are bound to have good ones there.'

We talked and our talk was a theme of kings,
A theme for strings. He hunkered down
In the shade of the orchard wall. O roses,
The old man dies in the young girl's frown.

And poet lost to potato-fields,
Remembering the lime and copper smell
Of the spraying barrels he is not lost
Or till blossomed stalks cannot weave a spell.

Donagh MacDonagh, 1947

MacDonagh defines 'this arrogant city' almost wholly in terms of what it is not.

Dublin Made Me

Dublin made me and no little town
With the country closing in on its streets,
The cattle walking proudly on its pavements,
The jobbers, the gombeenmen and the cheats

Devouring the fair-day between them
A public-house to half a hundred men
And the teacher, the solicitor and the bank-clerk
In the hotel bar, drinking for ten.

Dublin made me, not the secret poteen still,
The raw and hungry hills of the West,
The lean road flung over profitless bog
Where only a snipe could nest,

Where the sea takes its tithe of every boat.
Bawneen and currach have no allegiance of mine,
Nor the cute, self-deceiving talkers of the South
Who look to the East for a sign.

The soft and dreary midlands with their tame canals
Wallow between sea and sea, remote from adventure,
And Northward a far and fortified province
Crouches under the lash of arid censure.

I disclaim all fertile meadows, all tilled land,
The evil that grows from it and the good,
But the Dublin of old statutes, this arrogant city,
Stirs proudly and secretly in my blood.

The voice in 'Stony Grey Soil' is hard and celebratory at once. In his poem 'Innocence', Kavanagh writes: 'Ashamed of what I loved/I flung her from me and called her a ditch/Although she was smiling at me with violets.' In this poem's closing stanzas he recognizes those tensions and calmly admits how much he owes his birthplace.

Stony Grey Soil

O stony grey soil of Monaghan,
The laugh from my love you thieved;
You took the gay child of my passion
And gave me your clod-conceived.

You clogged the feet of my boyhood,
And I believed that my stumble
Had the poise and stride of Apollo
And his voice my thick-tongued mumble.

You told me the plough was immortal!
O green-life-conquering plough!
Your mandril strained, your coulter blunted
In the smooth lea-field of my brow.

You sang on steaming dunghills
A song of cowards' brood,
You perfumed my clothes with weasel itch,
You fed me on swinish food.

You flung a ditch on my vision
Of beauty, love and truth.
O stony grey soil of Monaghan,
You burgled my bank of youth!

Lost the long hours of pleasure,
All the women that love young men.
O can I still stroke the monster's back
Or write with unpoisoned pen

His name in these lonely verses,
Or mention the dark fields where
The first gay flight of my lyric
Got caught in a peasant's prayer.

Mullahinsha, Drummeril, Black Shanco –
Wherever I turn I see
In the stony grey soil of Monaghan
Dead loves that were born for me.

Kavanagh here describes a familiar, ordinary world and makes it his own, just as he does in *Tarry Flynn* when he says that 'The summer sun was going down in a most wonderful yellow ball behind the hills of Drumnay. It turned the dirty upstairs windows of Cassidy's house into stained glass.'

A Christmas Childhood

I

One side of the potato-pits was white with frost –
How wonderful that was, how wonderful!
And when we put our ears to the paling-post
The music that came out was magical.

The light between the ricks of hay and straw
Was a hole in Heaven's gable. An apple tree
With its December-glinting fruit we saw –
O you, Eve, were the world that tempted me

To eat the knowledge that grew in clay
And death the germ within it! Now and then
I can remember something of the gay
Garden that was childhood's. Again

The tracks of cattle to a drinking-place,
A green stone lying sideways in a ditch,
Or any common sight, the transfigured face
Of a beauty that the world did not touch.

II

My father played the melodion
Outside at our gate;
There were stars in the morning east
And they danced to his music.

Across the wild bogs his melodion called
To Lennons and Callans.
As I pulled on my trousers in a hurry
I knew some strange thing had happened.

Outside in the cow-house my mother
Made the music of milking;
The light of her stable-lamp was a star
And the frost of Bethlehem made it twinkle.

A water-hen screeched in the bog,
Mass-going feet
Crunched the wafer-ice on the pot-holes,
Somebody wistfully twisted the bellows wheel.

My child poet picked out the letters
On the grey stone,
In silver the wonder of a Christmas townland,
The winking glitter of a frosty dawn.

Cassiopeia was over
Cassidy's hanging hill,
I looked and three whin bushes rode across
The horizon – the Three Wise Kings.

An old man passing said:
'Can't he make it talk –
The melodion.' I hid in the doorway
And tightened the belt of my box-pleated coat.

I nicked six nicks on the door-post
With my penknife's big blade –
There was a little one for cutting tobacco.
And I was six Christmases of age.

My father played the melodion,
My mother milked the cows,
And I had a prayer like a white rose pinned
On the Virgin Mary's blouse.

The corncrake – now barely present in Ireland, owing to changes in land use and farming practices – favours hayfields, long weeds and drier bogs. Even when the corncrake was a fixture of the Irish countryside, it was rarely seen, and manifested itself mainly by the *kerrx-kerrx* call of the male.

First Corncrake

We heard the corncrake's call from close at hand,
and took the lane that led us near the noise;
a hedged half-acre, flanked by sycamore,
was his small wedge of world. We crouched and peered
through the close thorn. The moving cry again
swivelled our gaze. Time whispered in the leaves.
A tall ditch-grass blade rocked as a languid bee
brushed the dry sliver with a rasping wing.

In silence still we watched; a careless heel
smashing a twig husk, grating on the grit,
and winning for itself a warning glance.
Then, when strung patience seemed about to yawn
as if the world demanded leave to move
on its slung reeling pitch about the sun,
I saw a head, a narrow pointed head
stirring among the brown weed-mottled grass
as the monotonous and edgy voice
kept up its hard complaint. I held the spot
in a fixed gaze. The brown head disappeared,

was seen in seconds in another clump,
and for a blessed moment, full in sight
the brown bird, brighter than the book foresaw,
stood calling in a little pool of grass.
I moved a finger and you shared the joy
that chance till then had never offered us.

It would have been a little grief to know
this punctual cry each year, and yet grow old
without one glimpse of him that made the cry.
The heart still hankers for the rounded shape.

The Blasket Islands, five in all, lie south-west of the Dingle Peninsula. The largest, An Blascaod Mór (The Great Blasket), is also known as An tOileán Thiar (The Western Island). Behan, a young IRA man, became interested in West Kerry and the Blaskets through a fellow prisoner while incarcerated for attempting to murder two Garda detectives, and it was in prison that he learned Irish. Behan first visited the Great Blasket in 1947, and wrote this poem about a disappearing way of life in 1948, while back in prison. The translator, Seán Hewitt, says that 'this poem shows a gentle longing for an Ireland wildly unlike the poet's own, one removed from him not simply geographically, but also culturally and linguistically.'

Jackeen ag Caoineadh na mBlascaod
Do Sheán Ó Briain as Baile an Fheirtéaraigh

Beidh an fharraige mhór faoi luí gréine mar ghloine,
Gan bád faoi sheol ná comhartha beo ó dhuine
Ach an t-iolar órga deireanach thuas ar imeall
An domhain, thar an mBlascaod uaigneach luite . . .

An ghrian ina luí is scáth na hoíche á scaipeadh
Ar ardú ré is í ag taitneamh i bhfuacht trí scamaill,
A méara loma sínte síos ar thalamh
Ar thithe scriosta briste, truamhar folamh . . .

Faoi thost ach cleltí na n-éan ag cuimilt thar tonna
Buíoch as a bheith fillte, ceann i mbrollach faoi shonas,
Séideadh na gaoithe ag luascadh go bog leathdhorais
Is an teallach fuar fliuch, gan tine, gan teas, gan chosaint.

Mountjoy, Lúnasa 1948

A Jackeen Keens for the Blasket
Translated by Seán Hewitt

Sunset, and the wide sea will be laid out like glass,
no sailing boats or signs of life, just a last
eagle that glints on the world's edge, separate,
circling over the lonely, spent Blasket . . .

The sun sunk down, and nightshadows scattered
over the high moon, herself scaling
the ground with bare, outstretched fingers, cold
on the broken houses, the life's scaffold . . .

All silent but the birds' bellies sliding
over the waves, glad to be home, head tucked
snug in breast, the wind's breath rocking the door,
and the damp hearth, fireless, heatless, unwatched.

Clarke, taking the side of lovers who feel like outsiders in mid-century Catholic Ireland, strongly condemns an oppressive Church and State.

The Envy of Poor Lovers

Pity poor lovers who may not do what they please
With their kisses under a hedge, before a raindrop
Unhouses it; and astir from wretched centuries,
Bramble and briar remind them of the saints.

Her envy is the curtain seen at night-time,
Happy position that could change her name.
His envy – clasp of the married whose thoughts can be alike,
Whose nature flows without the blame or shame.

Lying in the grass as if it were a sin
To move, they hold each other's breath, tremble,
Ready to share that ancient dread – kisses begin
Again – of Ireland keeping company with them.

Think, children, of institutions mured above
Your ignorance, where every look is veiled,
State-paid to snatch away the folly of poor lovers
For whom, it seems, the sacraments have failed.

Patrick MacDonogh, who has been described by Derek Mahon as one of Ireland's most neglected poets, juxtaposes two ideas of Ireland and explores the dark flip-side of the country's ideas about itself.

O, Come to the Land

O, come to the land of the saint and the scholar
Where learning and piety live without quarrel,
Where the coinage of mind outvalues the dollar
And God is the immanent shaper of thought and behaviour;
Where old ceremonious usage survives as the moral
And actual pattern of grace, where the blood of our Saviour
Is real as our sin, and replenishes spirit and brain
Till they blossom in pity and love as our fields in the rain.

No, but come to a land where the secret censor
Snouts in the dark, where authority smothers
The infant conscience and shadows a denser
Darkness on ignorant minds in their tortuous groping
For spectreless day: a land where austerity mothers
The coldly deliberate sins, where harsh masters are roping
The heels of the heavenly horse and blinding the bright
Incorruptible eye that dares open in passionless light.

O, come to the land where man is yet master
Of tyrannous time and will pause for the pleasure
Of speech or of sport though worldly disaster
Pluck at torn sleeves; a land where soft voices

Meet answering laughter, where the business of living is
    leisure.
Where there's no heart so poor but it's kindly and quick and
    rejoices
In horse or in hound or the mettlesome boy with a ball,
Where a jibe's for the proud, but a hand's for the
    helpless from all.

No, but come to a land where the mediaeval
Dread of the woman mutters in corners,
Thunders from pulpits, where the only evil
Lacking forgiveness is love; a land where the spirit
Withers the flowering flesh, where whispering mourners
Crowd to the grave of romance and expect to inherit
Great scandalous wealth to lighten long evenings and bring
A venomous joy to harsh lips whose kiss is a sting.

O, come to the land where imagination
Fashions the speech of the common people
Rich as a tenement's shattered mouldings
Where the wrong of defeat has bequeathed to a nation
Ironic traditional wit, like a polished steeple
Rising precise and clear from the huddled holdings
Of intricate minds that, in face of Eternity, know
Harsh humour and absolute faith their sole strongholds
    below.

No, but come to a land where the dying eagle
Is mocked by the crow and the patient vulture,
Where nobility fails and the ancient regal

Pride of inheritance yields to the last invaders –
Image and hare-brained song, the scum of an alien culture
Bubbling in village and street, where unmannerly traders
And politic slaves have supplanted the gentle and brave,
Where the hero will never have honour except in the grave.

The farm that Kavanagh inherited consisted of seven watery north-facing hills, 'sharp, crooked and triangular, the triangularity providing the most efficient system for drainage. Shancoduff is the name of a townland and whenever you get the duff (or dubh) in a townland's name it means that the land faces north. It was sour land, lime deficient . . .' Yet in this poem the black hills have become 'My hills' and he loves them. Among his own poems, 'Shancoduff' was Kavanagh's favourite.

Shancoduff

My black hills have never seen the sun rising,
Eternally they look north towards Armagh.
Lot's wife would not be salt if she had been
Incurious as my black hills that are happy
When dawn whitens Glassdrummond chapel.

My hills hoard the bright shillings of March
While the sun searches in every pocket.
They are my Alps and I have climbed the Matterhorn
With a sheaf of hay for three perishing calves
In the field under the Big Forth of Rocksavage.

The sleety winds fondle the rushy beards of Shancoduff
While the cattle-drovers sheltering in the Featherna Bush
Look up and say: 'Who owns them hungry hills
That the water-hen and snipe must have forsaken?
A poet? Then by heavens he must be poor.'
I hear and is my heart not badly shaken?

Though Kavanagh's tribute to his mother tells of her death, it is a poem full of life and movement. Bridget Kavanagh died suddenly, aged seventy-three, on 10 November 1945, and, in a poem that was first published in the *Standard* just four weeks later, Kavanagh (who was for a time that paper's film critic) remembers her in a series of flowing, cinematic images.

In Memory of My Mother

I do not think of you lying in the wet clay
Of a Monaghan graveyard; I see
You walking down a lane among the poplars
On your way to the station, or happily

Going to second Mass on a summer Sunday –
You meet me and you say:
'Don't forget to see about the cattle –'
Among your earthiest words the angels stray.

And I think of you walking along a headland
Of green oats in June,
So full of repose, so rich with life –
And I see us meeting at the end of a town

On a fair day by accident, after
The bargains are all made and we can walk
Together through the shops and stalls and markets
Free in the oriental streets of thought.

O you are not lying in the wet clay,
For it is a harvest evening now and we
Are piling up the ricks against the moonlight
And you smile up at us – eternally.

The place we come from, with its particular language and names, remains with us wherever we go.

Kerr's Ass

We borrowed the loan of Kerr's big ass
To go to Dundalk with butter,
Brought him home the evening before the market
An exile that night in Mucker.

We heeled up the cart before the door,
We took the harness inside –
The straw-stuffed straddle, the broken breeching
With bits of bull-wire tied;

The winkers that had no choke-band,
The collar and the reins . . .
In Ealing Broadway, London Town,
I name their several names

Until a world comes to life –
Morning, the silent bog,
And the god of imagination waking
In a Mucker fog.

A row between two Monaghan farmers in 1938 inspired this poem, but, as Seamus Heaney pointed out, 'It is a poem more in praise of Kavanagh's idea of Homer than in praise of Kavanagh's home.'

Epic

I have lived in important places, times
When great events were decided: who owned
That half a rood of rock, a no-man's land
Surrounded by our pitchfork-armed claims.
I heard the Duffys shouting 'Damn your soul'
And old McCabe, stripped to the waist, seen
Step the plot defying blue cast-steel –
'Here is the march along these iron stones.'
That was the year of the Munich bother. Which
Was more important? I inclined
To lose my faith in Ballyrush and Gortin
Till Homer's ghost came whispering to my mind.
He said: I made the *Iliad* from such
A local row. Gods make their own importance.

Austin Clarke, 1963

Clarke was ahead of his time in this poem, engaging with the plight of young Irish women who became pregnant out of wedlock, and evoking the grim institutions where they and their children were housed and exploited.

Unmarried Mothers

In the convent of the Sacred Heart,
The Long Room has been decorated
Where a Bishop can dine off golden plate:
An Oriental Potentate.
Girls, who will never wheel a go-cart,
Cook, sew, wash, dig, milk cows, clean stables
And, twice a day, giving their babes
The teat, herdlike, yield milk that cost
Them dearly, when their skirts were tossed up
Above their haunches. Hook or zip
Has warded them at Castlepollard.
Luckier girls, on board a ship,
Watch new hope spraying from the bollard.

Born in County Laois, Cecil Day Lewis grew up in England; this poem remembers childhood trips to Ireland.

Fishguard to Rosslare

From all my childhood voyages back to Ireland
Only two things remembered: gulls afloat
Off Fishguard quay littering a patch of radiance
Shed by the midnight boat.

And at dawn a low, dun coast shaping to meet me,
An oyster sky opening above Rosslare . . .
I rub the sleep from my eyes. Gulls pace the moving
Mast-head. We're almost there.

Gulls white as a dream on the pitch of Fishguard harbour,
Paper cut-outs, birds on a lacquered screen;
The low coastline and the pearl sky of Ireland;
A long sleep in between.

A sleep between two waking dreams – the haven,
The landfall – is how it appears now. The child's eye,
Unpuzzled, saw plain facts: I catch a glint from
The darkness they're haunted by.

The world of 'Churning Day' lasted for centuries and then quickly disappeared. The churn in the home in which Heaney grew up, as he told Dennis O'Driscoll in *Stepping Stones*, stood 'in the middle of the kitchen floor – it was usually kept out in the scullery but there was no room in the scullery to get at the action. A plunge churn, hooped and lidded, the timber lid with a hole in the middle of it to let it down over the staff. It was hard work but social work, whoever was in the house giving a hand, needing to keep the slush and slap of it going.'

Churning Day

A thick crust, coarse-grained as limestone rough-cast,
hardened gradually on top of the four crocks
that stood, large pottery bombs, in the small pantry.
After the hot brewery of gland, cud and udder,
cool porous earthenware fermented the buttermilk
for churning day, when the hooped churn was scoured
with plumping kettles and the busy scrubber
echoed daintily on the seasoned wood.
It stood then, purified, on the flagged kitchen floor.

Out came the four crocks, spilled their heavy lip
of cream, their white insides, into the sterile churn.
The staff, like a great whiskey muddler fashioned
in deal wood, was plunged in, the lid fitted.
My mother took first turn, set up rhythms
that slugged and thumped for hours. Arms ached.
Hands blistered. Cheeks and clothes were spattered
with flabby milk.

Where finally gold flecks
began to dance. They poured hot water then,
sterilized a birchwood-bowl
and little corrugated butter-spades.
Their short stroke quickened, suddenly
a yellow curd was weighting the churned-up white,
heavy and rich, coagulated sunlight
that they fished, dripping, in a wide tin strainer,
heaped up like gilded gravel in the bowl.

The house would stink long after churning day,
acrid as a sulphur mine. The empty crocks
were ranged along the wall again, the butter
in soft printed slabs was piled on pantry shelves.
And in the house we moved with gravid ease,
our brains turned crystals full of clean deal churns,
the plash and gurgle of the sour-breathed milk,
the pat and slap of small spades on wet lumps.

Derek Mahon, 1968

Though far from home, the memory holds, stores and nourishes and provides perspective. Inis Oírr, though three thousand miles away, matters. Derek Mahon wrote this poem in Cambridge, Massachusetts.

Inis Oírr

For Eamon Grennan

A dream of limestone in sea-light
Where gulls have placed their perfect prints.
Reflection in that final sky
Shames vision into simple sight;
Into pure sense, experience.
Atlantic leagues away tonight,
Conceived beyond such innocence,
I clutch the memory still, and I
Have measured everything with it since.

Before his execution, in Pentonville, for high treason in 1916, Roger Casement expressed a wish to be buried in his native County Antrim. His remains were turned over to the Irish State in 1965, but only on the condition that they not be brought into Northern Ireland. Following a state funeral Casement's remains were buried in Glasnevin Cemetery in Dublin. Richard Murphy's poem, from his book-length sequence *The Battle of Aughrim*, interprets the Casement obsequies with a sympathetic but critical eye.

Casement's Funeral

After the noose, and the black diary deeds
Gossiped, his fame roots in prison lime:
The hanged bones burn, a revolution seeds.
Now Casement's skeleton is flying home.

A gun salutes, the troops slow-march, our new
Nation atones for her shawled motherland
Whose welcome gaoled him when a U-boat threw
This rebel Quixote soaked on Banna Strand.

Soldiers in green guard the draped catafalque
With chalk remains of once ambiguous bone
Which fathered nothing till the traitor's dock
Hurt him to tower in legend like Wolfe Tone.

From gaol yard to the Liberator's tomb
Pillared in frost, they carry the freed ash,
Transmuted relic of a death-cell flame
Which purged for martyrdom the diarist's flesh.

On the small screen I watch the packed cortège
Pace from High Mass. Rebels in silk hats now
Exploit the grave with an old comrade's speech:
White hair tossed, a black cape flecked with snow.

This is an unexpected sonnet: the couplet comes first, the three quatrains follow. Is the old woman, with rosary beads and black shawl, Mother Ireland?

'I saw magic on a green country road –'

I saw magic on a green country road –
that old woman, a bag of sticks her load,

blackly down to her thin feet a fringed shawl,
a rosary of bone on her horned hand,
a flight of curlews scribing by her head,
and ashtrees combing with their frills her hair.

Her eyes, wet sunken holes pierced by an awl,
must have deciphered her adoring land:
and curlews, no longer lean birds, instead
become ten scarlet comets in the air.

Some incantation from her canyoned mouth,
Irish, English, blew frost along the ground,
and even though the wind was from the south
the ash-leaves froze without an ash-leaf sound.

Ireland has become home to many invaders and immigrants who have, over the centuries, gone native.

A Warning to Conquerors

This is the country of the Norman tower,
The graceless keep, the bleak and slitted eye
Where fear drove comfort out; straw on the floor
Was price of conquering security.

They came and won, and then for centuries
Stood to their arms; the face grew bleak and lengthened
In the night vigil, while their foes at ease
Sang of the strangers and the towers they strengthened.

Ragweed and thistle hold the Norman field
And cows the hall where Gaelic never rang
Melodiously to harp or spinning wheel.
Their songs are spent now with the voice that sang;

And lost their conquest. This soft land quietly
Engulfed them like the Saxon and the Dane –
But kept the jutted brow, the slitted eye;
Only the faces and the names remain.

Heaney was born in 'a one-storey, longish, lowish, thatched and white-washed house' in 1939. Thatched roofs require maintenance and repair, and the expert thatcher was an important, valued, busy and much admired craftsman.

Thatcher

Bespoke for weeks, he turned up some morning
Unexpectedly, his bicycle slung
With a light ladder and a bag of knives.
He eyed the old rigging, poked at the eaves,

Opened and handled sheaves of lashed wheat-straw.
Next, the bundled rods: hazel and willow
Were flicked for weight, twisted in case they'd snap.
It seemed he spent the morning warming up:

Then fixed the ladder, laid out well-honed blades
And snipped at straw and sharpened ends of rods
That, bent in two, made a white-pronged staple
For pinning down his world, handful by handful.

Couchant for days on sods above the rafters,
He shaved and flushed the butts, stitched all together
Into a sloped honeycomb, a stubble patch,
And left them gaping at his Midas touch.

Empty, ruined villages can still be found in rural Ireland, reminders of a devastating time in our history. Ryan's poem evokes one such village on Achill Island.

Famine Village

This maze of stones which the wind cuts and hones
Smooth now, was in another century
The houses of famine fishermen, where bones

Long scattered, now without a memory,
Have fertilised this bramble wilderness
Of grass and thistle reaching to the knee,

Which press upward and thicken, and caress
The naked chimneys and the broken walls
Breathing the sea-mist and the emptiness.

Where once children played, now only gulls' calls
Echo and die slowly across the wide
Wild curve of sand to where the mountain falls

Into the sea. From the sick land they tried
To work the tide; they lived a life-long fight
To live and lost to graves on Slieve More's side.

Now a grey rain thickens the fading light.
Slowly the ruins become the mist and
Merge silently with the descending night.

An innocent, carefree scene becomes a horrific one. Egan's question answers itself.

The Northern Ireland Question

two *wee girls*
were playing tig near a car . . .

how many counties would you say
are worth their scattered fingers?

John Montague, 1972

Frank O'Connor, Sean Ó Faoláin and other mid-century literary figures advanced an influential critique of a joyless, priest-ridden country. Montague's poem – set in 1963, the year Pope John XXIII died – suggests that Ireland had, for good or ill, become more free; or had perhaps never been quite so constricted as that critique made out. The poem's refrain plays on Yeats's 'Romantic Ireland's dead and gone' from his poem 'September 1913'.

The Siege of Mullingar

At the Fleadh Cheoil in Mullingar
There were two sounds, the breaking
Of glass, and the background pulse
Of music. Young girls roamed
The streets with eager faces,
Shoving for men. Bottles in
Hand, they rowed out a song:
Puritan Ireland's dead and gone,
A myth of O'Connor and Ó Faoláin.

In the early morning the lovers
Lay on both sides of the canal
Listening on Sony transistors
To the agony of Pope John.
Yet it didn't seem strange, or blasphemous,
This ground bass of death and
Resurrection, as we strolled along:
Puritan Ireland's dead and gone,
A myth of O'Connor and Ó Faoláin.

Further on, breasting the wind
Waves of the deserted grain harbour,
A silent pair, a cob and his pen,
Most nobly linked. Everything then
In our casual morning vision
Seemed to flow in one direction,
Lines simple as a song:
Puritan Ireland's dead and gone,
A myth of O'Connor and Ó Faoláin.

Paul Durcan, 1975

This uncompromising two-line snapshot encapsulates the worst year of the Troubles, when 496 people were killed in Northern Ireland.

Ireland 1972

Next to the fresh grave of my belovèd grandmother
The grave of my first love murdered by my brother.

A cascade of images describes a complex personality. She is an unnamed woman, a Sean Bhean Bhocht and one who was only truly missed after she had died. The poem, shaped like a headstone, is Hartnett's memorial to an individual, a way of life, a vanished world.

Death of an Irishwoman

Ignorant, in the sense
she ate monotonous food
and thought the world was flat,
and pagan, in the sense
she knew the things that moved
at night were neither dogs not cats
but *púcas* and darkfaced men,
she nevertheless had fierce pride.
But sentenced in the end
to eat thin diminishing porridge
in a stone-cold kitchen
she clenched her brittle hands
around a world
she could not understand.
I loved her from the day she died.
She was a summer dance at the crossroads.
She was a card game where a nose was broken.
She was a song that nobody sings.
She was a house ransacked by soldiers.
She was a language seldom spoken.
She was a child's purse, full of useless things.

If this poem were pinned up above a sink or desk in Tokyo, Sydney, Los Angeles or Budapest, it would bring alive in the reader a place wild, unspoilt and in perpetual motion. It's an uninhabited Ireland; there is no trace anywhere of a human presence. Michael Longley has written that the poem's 'narrow shape on the page' works as 'a single shaft of sunlight breaking through on an overcast day'; and he describes 'Windharp' as 'a halting prayer, a broken spell'.

Windharp

For Patrick Collins

The sounds of Ireland,
that restless whispering
you never get away
from, seeping out of
low bushes and grass,
heatherbells and fern,
wrinkling bog pools,
scraping tree branches,
light hunting cloud,
sound hounding sight,
a hand ceaselessly
combing and stroking
the landscape, till
the valley gleams
like the pile upon
a mountain pony's coat.

McAuley was born in Dublin in 1936, emigrated to the US in 1966 and
retired to County Wicklow in 1998. 'Green Beer' arrestingly juxtaposes
Irish-American blarney with Ireland's new and ancient violence.

Green Beer

I

On Saint Paddy's Day, the jukebox plays
Bing Crosby singing 'Galway Bay',
And the color TV in this friendly dive
Is freckled with kilted dancers, live
Little dolls with their jigs and reels
Between the commercials for stomach pills.

The barman slides me another beer.
'On the house, Irish.' 'Good to be here.'
He asks me – they all ask – what I think.
I assure him the situation stinks.
'The murther and mayhem over there
Is somethin' a body can hardly bear,'
My brogue as phony as the beer is green.
The barman tops her up again.
The Gaelic lassies from the Bronx
Blur and fade as they end their dance.

II

I dream a flag snaps in a cold wind:
The Plough-stars in gold on a blue ground,
Blurred by smoke. Kneeling beneath,

A shadow, on watch: an armed youth,
Fist clenched over the burning town.
Into the red sky creeps a false dawn.
Then dead Cuchulain bound to the tree,
And the raven stabbing his eye.

Old roads disappear from view, they 'lose their grip', but Ní Chuilleanáin imagines their ghostly life.

Old Roads

Missing from the map, the abandoned roads
Reach across the mountain, threading into
Clefts and valleys, shuffle between thick
Hedges of flowery thorn.
The grass flows into tracks of wheels,
Mowed evenly by the careful sheep;
Drenched, it guards the gaps of silence
Only trampled on the pattern day.

And if, an odd time, late
At night, a cart passes
Splashing in a burst stream, crunching bones,
The wavering candle hung by the shaft
Slaps light against a single gable
Catches a flat tombstone
Shaking a nervous beam as the hare passes.

Their arthritic fingers
Their stiffening grasp cannot
Hold long on the hillside –
Slowly the old roads lose their grip.

Seamus Heaney, 1975

Heaney published this evocation of sectarian defiance in his 1975 collection *North*, a volume much concerned with the relationship between myth, ritual and violence.

Orange Drums, Tyrone, 1966

The lambeg balloons at his belly, weighs
Him back on his haunches, lodging thunder
Grossly there between his chin and his knees.
He is raised up by what he buckles under.

Each arm extended by a seasoned rod,
He parades behind it. And though the drummers
Are granted passage through the nodding crowd,
It is the drums preside, like giant tumours.

To every cocked ear, expert in its greed,
His battered signature subscribes 'No Pope'.
The goatskin's sometimes plastered with his blood.
The air is pounding like a stethoscope.

The title suggests something familiar, ordinary and local, but the poem becomes a meditation on the plight of people who have known suffering, injustice and catastrophe over many centuries.

A Disused Shed in Co. Wexford

Let them not forget us, the weak souls among the asphodels.
— Seferis, *Mythistorema*

For J. G. Farrell

Even now there are places where a thought might grow –
Peruvian mines, worked out and abandoned
To a slow clock of condensation,
An echo trapped for ever, and a flutter
Of wildflowers in the lift-shaft,
Indian compounds where the wind dances
And a door bangs with diminished confidence,
Lime crevices behind rippling rain-barrels,
Dog corners for bone burials;
And in a disused shed in Co. Wexford,

Deep in the grounds of a burnt-out hotel,
Among the bathtubs and the washbasins
A thousand mushrooms crowd to a keyhole.
This is the one star in their firmament
Or frames a star within a star.

What should they do there but desire?
So many days beyond the rhododendrons
With the world waltzing in its bowl of cloud,
They have learnt patience and silence
Listening to the rooks querulous in the high wood.

They have been waiting for us in a foetor
Of vegetable sweat since civil war days,
Since the gravel-crunching, interminable departure
Of the expropriated mycologist.
He never came back, and light since then
Is a keyhole rusting gently after rain.
Spiders have spun, flies dusted to mildew
And once a day, perhaps, they have heard something –
A trickle of masonry, a shout from the blue
Or a lorry changing gear at the end of the lane.

There have been deaths, the pale flesh flaking
Into the earth that nourished it;
And nightmares, born of these and the grim
Dominion of stale air and rank moisture.
Those nearest the door grow strong –
'Elbow room! Elbow room!'
The rest, dim in a twilight of crumbling
Utensils and broken pitchers, groaning
For their deliverance, have been so long
Expectant that there is left only the posture.

A half century, without visitors, in the dark –
Poor preparation for the cracking lock

And creak of hinges; magi, moonmen,
Powdery prisoners of the old regime,
Web-throated, stalked like triffids, racked by drought
And insomnia, only the ghost of a scream
At the flash-bulb firing-squad we wake them with
Shows there is life yet in their feverish forms.
Grown beyond nature now, soft food for worms,
They lift frail heads in gravity and good faith.

They are begging us, you see, in their wordless way,
To do something, to speak on their behalf
Or at least not to close the door again.
Lost people of Treblinka and Pompeii!
'Save us, save us,' they seem to say,
'Let the god not abandon us
Who have come so far in darkness and in pain.
We too had our lives to live.
You with your light meter and relaxed itinerary,
Let not our naive labours have been in vain!'

Durcan suggests that there is no contradiction between sexual liber-
ation and a rich sense of Irishness – but an elderly Eamon de Valera
disagrees.

Making Love Outside Áras an Uachtaráin

When I was a boy, myself and my girl
Used bicycle up to the Phoenix Park;
Outside the gates we used lie in the grass
Making love outside Áras an Uachtaráin.

Often I wondered what de Valera would have thought
Inside in his ivory tower
If he knew that we were in his green, green grass
Making love outside Áras an Uachtaráin.

Because the odd thing was – oh how odd it was –
We both revered Irish patriots
And we dreamed our dreams of a green, green flag
Making love outside Áras an Uachtaráin.

But even had our names been Diarmaid and Gráinne
We doubted de Valera's approval
For a poet's son and a judge's daughter
Making love outside Áras an Uachtaráin.

I see him now in the heat-haze of the day
Blindly stalking us down;
And, levelling an ancient rifle, he says 'Stop
Making love outside Áras an Uachtaráin.'

De Valera, a towering presence in Ireland for decades, died on 29 August 1975, aged ninety-two. In Thomas McCarthy's poem, de Valera's death highlights the gap between two Irelands, old and young.

State Funeral

Parnell will never come again, he said. He's there, all that was mortal of him. Peace to his ashes.

　　　　　　　　　　　　　　　　　– James Joyce, *Ulysses*

That August afternoon the family
Gathered. There was a native *déjà vu*
Of Funeral when we settled against the couch
On our sunburnt knees. We gripped mugs of tea
Tightly and soaked the TV spectacle;
The boxed ritual in our living room.

My father recited prayers of memory,
Of monster meetings, blazing tar-barrels
Planted outside Free-State homes, the Broy-
Harriers pushing through a crowd, Blueshirts;
And, after the war, de Valera's words
Making Churchill's imperial palette blur.

What I remember is one decade of darkness,
A mind-stifling boredom; long summers
For blackberry picking and churning cream,

Winters for saving timber and setting lines
And snares: none of the joys of here and now
With its instant jam, instant heat and cream:

It was a landscape for old men. Today
They lowered the tallest one, tidied him
Away while his people watched quietly.
In the end he had retreated to the first dream,
Caning truth. I think of his austere grandeur;
Taut sadness, like old heroes he had imagined.

The Ireland Ormsby knew was intensely mindful of its dark, violent past; but he prefers to celebrate a history of purely personal significance.

A Small Town in Ireland

The road runs into it and out
    About the bridge the people go.
Someone was executed there,
    (Was it two hundred years ago?)

Is sung of still. But I would sing
    A roof, a door, a set of bricks,
Because you entered Ireland there
    One night in nineteen forty-six.

These are the rails your fingers touched
    Passing to school, the waves below
You dipped your toes in. That is all
    The history I would want to know,

Were not the waters those that eyes
    Had flung their final glance upon,
Coursing, untouched and blameless, past the loss
    Of someone's lover, someone's son.

Thirteen demonstrators were killed by British forces on Bloody Sunday, 30 January 1972, in Derry city. Three days later, a Requiem Mass was held for eleven of the thirteen. Devlin's pub in Ardboe, County Tyrone – owned by Seamus Heaney's father-in-law – closed early that night, observing a republican paramilitary curfew. Louis O'Neill, a fisherman and a regular at Devlin's, went instead to a pub that hadn't observed the curfew and was killed by a bomb placed there. Heaney said that the metre in Yeats's 1914 poem 'The Fisherman' was a 'tuning fork' for 'Casualty'.

Casualty

I

He would drink by himself
And raise a weathered thumb
Towards the high shelf,
Calling another rum
And blackcurrant, without
Having to raise his voice,
Or order a quick stout
By a lifting of the eyes
And a discreet dumb-show
Of pulling off the top;
At closing time would go
In waders and peaked cap
Into the showery dark,
A dole-kept breadwinner
But a natural for work.
I loved his whole manner,

Sure-footed but too sly,
His deadpan sidling tact,
His fisherman's quick eye
And turned, observant back.

Incomprehensible
To him, my other life.
Sometimes, on his high stool,
Too busy with his knife
At a tobacco plug
And not meeting my eye,
In the pause after a slug
He mentioned poetry.
We would be on our own
And, always politic
And shy of condescension,
I would manage by some trick
To switch the talk to eels
Or lore of the horse and cart
Or the Provisionals.

But my tentative art
His turned back watches too:
He was blown to bits
Out drinking in a curfew
Others obeyed, three nights
After they shot dead
The thirteen men in Derry.
PARAS THIRTEEN, the walls said,
BOGSIDE NIL. That Wednesday

Everybody held
Their breath and trembled.

II

It was a day of cold
Raw silence, windblown
Surplice and soutane:
Rained-on, flower-laden
Coffin after coffin
Seemed to float from the door
Of the packed cathedral
Like blossoms on slow water.
The common funeral
Unrolled its swaddling band,
Lapping, tightening
Till we were braced and bound
Like brothers in a ring.

But he would not be held
At home by his own crowd
Whatever threats were phoned,
Whatever black flags waved.
I see him as he turned
In that bombed offending place,
Remorse fused with terror
In his still knowable face,
His cornered outfaced stare
Blinding in the flash.

He had gone miles away
For he drank like a fish
Nightly, naturally
Swimming towards the lure
Of warm lit-up places,
The blurred mesh and murmur
Drifting among glasses
In the gregarious smoke.
How culpable was he
That last night when he broke
Our tribe's complicity?
'Now you're supposed to be
An educated man,'
I hear him say. 'Puzzle me
The right answer to that one.'

III

I missed his funeral,
Those quiet walkers
And sideways talkers
Shoaling out of his lane
To the respectable
Purring of the hearse . . .
They move in equal pace
With the habitual
Slow consolation
Of a dawdling engine,
The line lifted, hand
Over fist, cold sunshine
On the water, the land

Banked under fog: that morning
When he took me in his boat,
The screw purling, turning
Indolent fathoms white,
I tasted freedom with him.
To get out early, haul
Steadily off the bottom,
Dispraise the catch, and smile
As you find a rhythm
Working you, slow mile by mile,
Into your proper haunt
Somewhere, well out, beyond . . .

Dawn-sniffing revenant,
Plodder through midnight rain,
Question me again.

Martin McBirney, QC and magistrate, was in Longley's words 'an all-Ireland man, a hail-fellow-well-met man, an egalitarian'. McBirney once invited a man who was mending the garage roof next door to have a cup of tea; what McBirney did not know was that the worker was an IRA member. A few days later the man returned and shot McBirney. 'The Civil Servant' is the first of three elegies in a sequence called 'Wreaths'.

The Civil Servant

He was preparing an Ulster fry for breakfast
When someone walked into the kitchen and shot him:
A bullet entered his mouth and pierced his skull,
The books he had read, the music he could play.

He lay in his dressing gown and pyjamas
While they dusted the dresser for fingerprints
And then shuffled backwards across the garden
With notebooks, cameras and measuring tapes.

They rolled him up like a red carpet and left
Only a bullet hole in the cutlery drawer:
Later his widow took a hammer and chisel
And removed the black keys from his piano.

Paul Muldoon, 1980

The Northern Ireland Troubles, as Muldoon observes in this poem, cast a sinister pall over ordinary scenes and situations.

Ireland

The Volkswagen parked in the gap,
But gently ticking over.
You wonder if it's lovers
And not men hurrying back
Across two fields and a river.

In this poem, Muldoon traces a boy's progression from primary school truant to IRA Commandant. Having being put in his place as a boy, he becomes a leader of men, in a disciplined revolutionary army.

Anseo

When the Master was calling the roll
At the primary school in Collegelands,
You were meant to call back *Anseo*
And raise your hand
As your name occurred.
Anseo, meaning here, here and now,
All present and correct,
Was the first word of Irish I spoke.
The last name on the ledger
Belonged to Joseph Mary Plunkett Ward
And was followed, as often as not,
By silence, knowing looks,
A nod and a wink, the Master's droll
'And where's our little Ward-of-court?'

I remember the first time he came back
The Master had sent him out
Along the hedges
To weigh up for himself and cut
A stick with which he would be beaten.
After a while, nothing was spoken;
He would arrive as a matter of course

With an ash-plant, a salley-rod.
Or, finally, the hazel-wand
He had whittled down to a whip-lash,
Its twist of red and yellow lacquers
Sanded and polished,
And altogether so delicately wrought
That he had engraved his initials on it.

I last met Joseph Mary Plunkett Ward
In a pub just over the Irish border.
He was living in the open,
In a secret camp
On the other side of the mountain.
He was fighting for Ireland,
Making things happen.
And he told me, Joe Ward,
Of how he had risen through the ranks
To Quartermaster, Commandant:
How every morning at parade
His volunteers would call back *Anseo*
And raise their hands
As their names occurred.

Mahon once referred to his most celebrated poem, 'A Disused Shed in Co. Wexford', as 'a grandiose bit of rhetoric'. He prefers the 'Garage', 'also grandiose but somehow less annoyingly so, I think'. The voice is inviting and welcoming when, in a memorable iambic pentameter, it asks us to recognize in a quiet corner of County Cork a place that is remembered by many emigrants: 'Somebody somewhere thinks of this as home.' The poem expresses a deep belief in the importance not of elsewhere but of the place where we come from.

A Garage in Co. Cork

Surely you paused at this roadside oasis
In your nomadic youth, and saw the mound
Of never-used cement, the curious faces,
The soft-drink ads and the uneven ground
Rainbowed with oily puddles, where a snail
Had scrawled its pearly, phosphorescent trail.

Like a frontier store-front in an old western
It might have nothing behind it but thin air,
Building materials, fruit boxes, scrap iron,
Dust-laden shrubs and coils of rusty wire,
A cabbage-white fluttering in the sodden
Silence of an untended kitchen garden –

Nirvana! But the cracked panes reveal a dark
Interior echoing with the cries of children.
Here in this quiet corner of Co. Cork

A family ate, slept, and watched the rain
Dance clean and cobalt the exhausted grit
So that the mind shrank from the glare of it.

Where did they go? South Boston? Cricklewood?
Somebody somewhere thinks of this as home,
Remembering the old pumps where they stood,
Antique now, squirting juice into a cream
Lagonda or a dung-caked tractor while
A cloud swam on a cloud-reflecting tile.

Surely a whitewashed sun-trap at the back
Gave way to hens, wild thyme, and the first few
Shadowy yards of an overgrown cart track,
Tyres in the branches such as Noah knew –
Beyond, a swoop of mountain where you heard,
Disconsolate in the haze, a single blackbird.

Left to itself, the functional will cast
A deathbed glow of picturesque abandon.
The intact antiquities of the recent past,
Dropped from the retail catalogues, return
To the materials that gave rise to them
And shine with a late sacramental gleam.

A god who spent the night here once rewarded
Natural courtesy with eternal life –
Changing to petrol pumps, that they be spared
For ever there, an old man and his wife.
The virgin who escaped his dark design
Sanctions the townland from her prickly shrine.

We might be anywhere but are in one place only,
One of the milestones of Earth-residence
Unique in each particular, the thinly
Peopled hinterland serenely tense –
Not in the hope of a resplendent future
But with a sure sense of its intrinsic nature.

From an island off Ireland's west coast, Harry Clifton considers his place in the world. At summer's end, he and his girl are, for the moment, free from history. 'Over there . . .' are laws, regulations, the weight of the past, adulthood.

Ireland

Offshore, islanded
On a sleepless night
At summer's end, this girl and I
Look across at Ireland
As we lie . . .

The law ends,
And the sense of time
Over there . . . it's a sheltered lee,
Our unsuperintended
Eternity.

Wild seed,
Warrens of breeding
Everywhere . . . on the Atlantic side
Graveyards of joyrides,
Used cars.

A ferry
Left some hours ago
For the mainland . . . nothing to carry us

Back into history, now,
Until tomorrow.

Moonless
Tides black out the piles
Of the landing-stage . . . phosphorescent
Plash of smiles
In darkness

Plays
Between us, in silence
Of fondling, young points growing
Tenderer in violence,
Responding,

But no breakthrough
Into adulthood, no release –
Only merchantmen, destroyers
Riding the breeze
At anchor,

And lights
Across the strait
Winking, calling our adolescence
Into question, as overnight
Ireland waits.

In Ballymoney, County Wexford, the speaker, 'here at the window', observing the cycles and rhythms of life, tells us very little about himself. And yet he tells us everything.

Facts of Life, Ballymoney

I would like to let things be:

the rain comes down on the roof,
the small birds come to the feeder,
the waves come slowly up the strand.

Three sounds to measure
my hour here at the window:
the slow swish of the sea,
the squeak of hungry birds,
the quick ticking of rain.

Then of course there are the trees –
bare for the most part.
The grass wide open to the rain,
clouds accumulating over the sea,
the water rising and falling and rising,
herring-gulls bobbing on the water.

They are killing cuttlefish out there,
one at a time without fuss.
With a brisk little shake of the head
they rinse their lethal beaks.

Rain-swollen, the small stream
twists between slippery rocks.
That's all there's to it, spilling
its own sound onto the sand.

In one breath, one wink, all this
melts to an element in my blood.
And still it's possible to go on
simply living
as if nothing had happened.

Nothing has happened:
rain inching down the window,
me looking out at the rain.

The Irish Constitution establishes the Irish language as the first official language of the state. A nationwide survey, in 1983, discovered that 66 per cent of those surveyed believed that 'Ireland would not really be Ireland without its Irish-speaking people'; 40 per cent agreed with the statement 'Irish is a dead language'. Aidan Mathews's succinct poem contains thirty-one reminders of the Irish-language word hoard.

The Death of Irish

The tide gone out for good,
Thirty-one words for seaweed whiten on the foreshore.

A selection of four poems from Hartnett's melancholy sequence of eighty-seven *Inchicore Haiku*. Number 82 brings to mind the old saying 'Saol fada agus bás in Éirinn' – 'Long life to you and may you die in Ireland.'

25

From St Michael's Church
the electric Angelus –
another job gone.

37

What do bishops take
when the price of bread goes up?
A vow of silence.

55

Along Emmet Road
politicians' promises
blow like plastic bags.

82

Dying in exile.
To die without a people
is the real death.

Kinsale's dramatic history – which includes its occupation by the Spanish in 1601 and the ensuing Battle of Kinsale – is not remembered here. The speaking voice contrasts a dark Ireland of church and bogland with an apparently brighter, affluent one.

Kinsale

The kind of rain we knew is a thing of the past –
deep-delving, dark, deliberate you would say,
browsing on spire and bogland; but today
our sky-blue slates are steaming in the sun,
our yachts tinkling and dancing in the bay
like racehorses. We contemplate at last
shining windows, a future forbidden to no one.

There are about three thousand holy wells in Ireland – of pagan origin, in many cases, but now dedicated to the Virgin Mary or local saints. This is the third part of Dunne's poem 'West Cork'.

Holy Well

The same tin cup for years but the rim
never spread the hurt that touched it.
Coins glitter in its depths like foil.
The water shivers at the mildest gust.
Pinched by midges, it trembles slightly.

Most of us see Government Buildings on the news or through high railings. Through the eyes of a cleaner, Paul Durcan brings us right to the Cabinet table.

The Cabinet Table

Alice Gunn is a cleaner woman
Down at Government Buildings,
And after seven o'clock Mass last night
(Isn't it a treat to be able to go to Sunday Mass
On a Saturday! To sit down to Saturday Night TV
Knowing you've fulfilled your Sunday obligation!)
She came back over to The Flats for a cup of tea
(I offered her sherry but she declined –
Oh, I never touch sherry on a Saturday night –
Whatever she meant by that, I don't know).
She had us in stitches, telling us
How one afternoon after a Cabinet Meeting
She got one of the security men
To lie down on the Cabinet Table,
And what she didn't do to him –
And what she did do to him –
She didn't half tell us;
But she told us enough to be going on with.
'Do you know what it is?' she says to me:
'No,' says I, 'what is it?'
'It's mahogany,' she says, 'pure mahogany.'

Fiacc, who referred to his native Belfast as 'Hellfast' and said 'you can't live here without being poisoned', in this poem portrays the poison of violence and fear.

Enemy Encounter

For Lilac

Dumping (left over from the autumn)
Dead leaves, near a culvert
I come on
            a British Army Soldier
With a rifle and a radio
Perched hiding. He has red hair.

He is young enough to be my weenie
-bopper daughter's boy-friend.
He is like a lonely little winter robin.
We are that close to each other, I
Can nearly hear his heart beating.

I say something bland to make him grin,
But his glass eyes look past my side
-whiskers down
                  the Shore Road street.
I am an Irish man
                  and he is afraid
That I have come to kill him.

This poem was written, Boland tells us, 'on a dining-room table, look-
ing out at a garden in spring when my children were small' and 'it tries
to describe a real displacement.' A woman in comfortable suburbia
remembers the Irish who emigrated, endured much and were forgotten.

The Emigrant Irish

Like oil lamps we put them out the back,

of our houses, of our minds. We had lights
better than, newer than and then

a time came, this time and now
we need them. Their dread, makeshift example.

They would have thrived on our necessities.
What they survived we could not even live.
By their lights now it is time to
imagine how they stood there, what they stood with,
that their possessions may become our power.

Cardboard. Iron. Their hardships parcelled in them.
Patience. Fortitude. Long-suffering
in the bruise-coloured dusk of the New World.

And all the old songs. And nothing to lose.

In this poem, Ciaran Carson develops an elegant metaphor for the chaos of the Troubles.

Belfast Confetti

Suddenly as the riot squad moved in, it was raining exclamation
    marks,
Nuts, bolts, nails, car-keys. A fount of broken type. And the
    explosion
Itself – an asterisk on the map. The hyphenated line, a burst
    of rapid fire . . .
I was trying to complete a sentence in my head, but it kept
    stuttering,
All the alleyways and side-streets blocked with stops and
    colons.

I know this labyrinth so well – Balaclava, Raglan, Inkerman,
    Odessa Street –
Why can't I escape? Every move is punctuated. Crimea Street.
    Dead end again.
A Saracen, Kremlin-2 mesh. Makrolon face-shields.
    Walkie-talkies. What is
My name? Where am I coming from? Where am I
    going? A fusillade of question-marks.

Tom Creedon, a footballer from Macroom, died aged twenty-nine while saving his son's life and the lives of other children who were in the path of a van that began rolling down a hill. O'Donoghue's poem remembers Creedon in full flight and evokes the excitement and pleasure of a big GAA day.

Munster Final

In memory of Tom Creedon, died 28 August 1983

The jarveys to the west side of the town
Are robbers to a man, and if you tried
To drive through The Gap, they'd nearly strike you
With their whips. So we parked facing for home
And joined the long troop down the meadowsweet-
And woodbine-scented road into the town.
By blue Killarney's lakes and glens to see
The white posts on the green! To be deafened
By the muzzy megaphone of Jimmy Shand
And the testy bray to keep the gangways clear.

As for Tom Creedon, I can see him still.
His back arching casually to field and clear.
'Glory Macroom! Good boy, Tom Creedon!'
We'd be back next year to try our luck in Cork.

We will be back next year, roaring ourselves
Hoarse, praying for better luck. After first Mass
We'll get there early; that's our only hope.
Keep clear of the carparks so we're not hemmed in,
And we'll be home, God willing, for the cows.

This is the third sonnet of Heaney's sequence 'Clearances'. In Sonnet 7
of the same sequence, Heaney writes of how he felt at his mother's
bedside when she was dying: 'The space we stood around had been
emptied/Into us to keep, it penetrated/Clearances that suddenly stood
open./High cries were felled and a pure change happened.' That space
is delineated throughout the sequence and especially in this sonnet,
which is remarkable for its quietness and intimacy.

'When all the others were away at Mass'

When all the others were away at Mass
I was all hers as we peeled potatoes.
They broke the silence, let fall one by one
Like solder weeping off the soldering iron:
Cold comforts set between us, things to share
Gleaming in a bucket of clean water.
And again let fall. Little pleasant splashes
From each other's work would bring us to our senses.

So while the parish priest at her bedside
Went hammer and tongs at the prayers for the dying
And some were responding and some crying
I remembered her head bent towards my head,
Her breath in mine, our fluent dipping knives –
Never closer the whole rest of our lives.

The US census records that there are now five times more Irish Americans in the States than there are people living in Ireland. Michael Coady's poem tells of a search for ghosts in Connecticut.

Assembling the Parts

Standing in sunshine
by Highway 84
I'm photographing a factory
which is no longer there

looking for my father
by an assembly line
which has halted
and vanished into air

catching the sepia ghost
of a young tubercular Irishman
who's left a rooming house
at 6 a.m. in a winter time
during the Depression

when my mother is still a girl
playing precocious violin,
a Miraculous Medal under
her blouse, in Protestant
oratorios in Waterford.

A pallid face in the crowd
in a dark winter time
he's coughing in the cold,
assembling typewriters
in Hartford, Connecticut,

waiting for blood on his pillow
to send him home, where he'll
meet her one ordinary
night with the band playing
Solitude in the Foresters' Hall.

Fifty years on
he's nine Septembers dead
and a tourist in sunshine
by Highway 84
is photographing a factory
which is no longer there,

assembling the parts
of the mundane mystery,
the common enigma of journeys
and unscheduled destinations,

the lost intersections
of person and place and time
uniquely fathering everyman
out of the random dark.

Nuala Ní Dhomhnaill knows that the Irish language is vulnerable, but hopes in this poem that it might find safe harbour. Angela Bourke says of this poem that 'The plants mentioned here . . . are Irish with names which themselves are full of poetry, like *coigeal na mban sí*, the fairy-woman's spindle for bulrush.'

Ceist na Teangan

Cuirim mo dhóchas ar snámh
i mbáidín teangan
faoi mar a leagfá naíonán
i gcliabhán
a bheadh fite fuaite
de dhuilleoga feileastraim
is bitiúman agus pic
bheith cuimilte lena thóin

ansan é a leagadh síos
i measc na ngiolcach
is coigeal na mban sí
le taobh na habhann,
féachaint n'fheadaraís
cá dtabharfaidh an sruth é,
féachaint, dála Mhaoise,
an bhfóirfidh iníon Fhorainn?

The Language Issue

Translated by Paul Muldoon

I place my hope on the water
in this little boat
of the language, the way a body might put
an infant

in a basket of intertwined
iris leaves,
its underside proofed
with bitumen and pitch,

then set the whole thing down amidst
the sedge
and bulrushes by the edge
of a river

only to have it borne hither and thither,
not knowing where it might end up;
in the lap, perhaps,
of some Pharaoh's daughter.

The details in Strong's poem are so vivid, the sensations so immediate, that it reads as if it must have been written out of doors, there and then, high up, in a blazing wind.

Beara Peninsula

There we are. See us now, high. Shock:
we cling, clutch in the bladed furze.
Fastnet far, flung on a foaming rock
in a wide empty water – a kind of fear:

that foaming band pulls down –
look up! that empty sea
charged full from wind and moon
compels our eye – oh up! look up!

What are we doing here with our mouths
laughing like the yellow gorse,
our skin in ecstasy as heather curves
to the windy clouds?

Michael Gorman, who was born in 1952 and brought up in County Sligo, vividly evokes the mental climate in which he was raised.

The People I Grew Up with Were Afraid

The people I grew up with were afraid.
They were alone too long in waiting-rooms,
in dispensaries and in offices whose functions
they did not understand.

To buck themselves up, they thought
of lost causes, of 'Nature-boy'
O'Dea who tried to fly
from his bedroom window;
of the hunch-backed, little typist
who went roller-skating at Strandhill.
Or, they re-lived the last afternoon
of Benny Kirwan, pale, bald,
Protestant shop-assistant in Lydons' drapery.
One Wednesday, the town's half-day,
he hanged himself from a tree
on the shore at Lough Gill.

And what were they afraid of? Rent
collectors, rate collectors, insurance men.
Things to do with money. But,
especially of their vengeful God.
On her death-bed, Ena Phelan prayed
that her son would cut his hair.

Sometimes, they return to me,
Summer lunchtimes, colcannon
for the boys, back-doors
of all the houses open, the
news blaring on the radios.
Our mother's factory pay-packet
is sitting in the kitchen press
and our father, without
humour or relief, is
waiting for the sky to fall.

Brendan Kennelly, 1991

Kennelly uses black humour and a jaunty rhythm to portray inner-city deprivation and a young girl lost to childhood. The broken rhyme scheme signals a broken world.

Eily Kilbride

On the north side of Cork city
Where I sported and played
On the banks of my own lovely Lee
Having seen the goat break loose in Grand Parade

I met a child, Eily Kilbride
Who'd never heard of marmalade,
Whose experience of breakfast
Was coldly limited,

Whose entire school day
Was a bag of crisps,
Whose parents had no work to do,

Who went, once, into the countryside,
Saw a horse with a feeding bag over its head
And thought it was sniffing glue.

In this powerful incantation, litanies of joy and healing frame an atrocity.

The Ice-Cream Man

Rum and raisin, vanilla, butter-scotch, walnut, peach:
You would rhyme off the flavours. That was before
They murdered the ice-cream man on the Lisburn Road
And you bought carnations to lay outside his shop.
I named for you all the wild flowers of the Burren
I had seen in one day: thyme, valerian, loosestrife,
Meadowsweet, tway blade, crowfoot, ling, angelica,
Herb robert, marjoram, cow parsley, sundew, vetch,
Mountain avens, wood sage, ragged robin, stitchwort,
Yarrow, lady's bedstraw, bindweed, bog pimpernel.

The biggest of the Blasket islands in County Kerry, the Great Blasket, was inhabited by a small Irish-speaking population until 1953, when the last islanders – much depleted by migration – were resettled on the mainland. Julie O'Callaghan casts a cold eye on the sentiments of returning emigrants.

The Great Blasket Island

Six men born on this island
have come back after twenty-one years.
They climb up the overgrown roads
to their family houses
and come out shaking their heads.
The roofs have fallen in,
birds have nested in the rafters.
All the whitewashed rooms
all the nagging and praying
and scolding and giggling
and crying and gossiping
are scattered in the memories of these men.
One says, 'Ten of us, blown to the winds –
some in England, some in America, some in Dublin.
Our whole way of life – extinct.'
He blinks back the tears
and looks across the island
past the ruined houses, the cliffs
and out to the horizon.

Listen, mister, most of us cry sooner or later
over a Great Blasket Island of our own.

In January 1984 Ann Lovett, a fifteen-year-old girl, gave birth in secret to her baby son at the Marian grotto on the outskirts of her home town of Granard, County Longford. She was found by passers-by, but by then the baby was dead, and she herself died later that day in hospital. A whole generation still remembers her name and the awful sadness and heartbreak associated with her story. Paula Meehan evokes this young woman and the harsh world she lived in through the voice of another young woman who experienced a strange, troubled pregnancy.

The Statue of the Virgin at Granard Speaks

It can be bitter here at times like this,
November wind sweeping across the border.
Its seeds of ice would cut you to the quick.
The whole town tucked up safe and dreaming,
even wild things gone to earth, and I
stuck up here in this grotto, without as much as
star or planet to ease my vigil.

The howling won't let up. Trees
cavort in agony as if they would be free
and take off – ghost voyagers
on the wind that carries intimations
of garrison towns, walled cities, ghetto lanes
where men hunt each other and invoke
the various names of God as blessing
on their death tactics, their night manoeuvres.
Closer to home the wind sails over

dying lakes. I hear fish drowning.
I taste the stagnant water mingled
with turf smoke from outlying farms.

They call me Mary – Blessed, Holy, Virgin.
They fit me to a myth of a man crucified:
the scourging and the falling, and the falling again,
the thorny crown, the hammer blow of iron
into wrist and ankle, the sacred bleeding heart.

They name me Mother of all this grief
though mated to no mortal man.
They kneel before me and their prayers
fly up like sparks from a bonfire
that blaze a moment, then wink out.

It can be lovely here at times. Springtime,
early summer. Girls in Communion frocks
pale rivals to the riot in the hedgerows
of cow parsley and haw blossom, the perfume
from every rushy acre that's left for hay
when the light swings longer with the sun's push north.

Or the grace of a midsummer wedding
when the earth herself calls out for coupling
and I would break loose of my stony robes,
pure blue, pure white, as if they had robbed
a child's sky for their colour. My being
cries out to be incarnate, incarnate,
maculate and tousled in a honeyed bed.

Even an autumn burial can work its own pageantry.
The hedges heavy with the burden of fruiting
crab, sloe, berry, hip; clouds scud east
pear scented, windfalls secret in long
orchard grasses, and some old soul is lowered
to his kin. Death is just another harvest
scripted to the season's play.

But on this All Souls' Night there is
no respite from the keening of the wind.
I would not be amazed if every corpse came risen
from the graveyard to join in exaltation with the gale,
a cacophony of bone imploring sky for judgement
and release from being the conscience of the town.

On a night like this I remember the child
who came with fifteen summers to her name,
and she lay down alone at my feet
without midwife or doctor or friend to hold her hand
and she pushed her secret out into the night,
far from the town tucked up in little scandals,
bargains struck, words broken, prayers, promises,
and though she cried out to me in extremis
I did not move,
I didn't lift a finger to help her,
I didn't intercede with heaven,
nor whisper the charmed word in God's ear.

On a night like this I number the days to the solstice
and the turn back to the light.

O sun,
centre of our foolish dance,
burning heart of stone,
molten mother of us all,
hear me and have pity.

A woman remembers her much younger self leaving the Aran Islands
for an enclosed life in a convent. On the morning she entered she saw
her first motor car, signalling a new and noisier Ireland.

A Nun Takes the Veil

That morning early I ran through briars
To catch the calves that were bound for market.
I stopped the once, to watch the sun
Rising over Doolin across the water.

The calves were tethered outside the house
While I had my breakfast: the last one at home
For forty years. I had what I wanted (they said
I could), so we'd loaf bread and Marie biscuits.

We strung the calves behind the boat,
Me keeping clear to protect my style:
Confirmation suit and my patent sandals.
But I trailed my fingers in the cool green water,

Watching the puffins driving homeward
To their nests on Aran. On the Galway mainland
I tiptoed clear of the cow-dunged slipway
And watched my brothers heaving the calves

As they lost their footing. We went in a trap,
Myself and my mother, and I said goodbye

To my father then. The last I saw of him
Was a hat and jacket and a salley stick,

Driving cattle to Ballyvaughan.
He died (they told me) in the country home,
Asking to see me. But that was later:
As we trotted on through the morning mist,

I saw a car for the first time ever,
Hardly seeing it before it vanished.
I couldn't believe it, and I stood up looking
To where I could hear its noise departing

But it was only a glimpse. That night in the convent
The sisters spoilt me, but I couldn't forget
The morning's vision, and I fell asleep
With the engine humming through the open window.

The golden eagle, once extinct, has reappeared in Donegal. Matthew Sweeney, who was born there, celebrates the return of the eagle and tells of how his father uses the Irish language to honour 'what used to be' and 'what is again'.

The Eagle

My father is writing in Irish.
The English language, with all its facts
will not do. It is too modern.
It is good for plane-crashes, for unemployment,
but not for the unexplained return
of the eagle to Donegal.

He describes the settled pair
in their eyrie on the not-so-high mountain.
He uses an archaic Irish
to describe what used to be, what is again,
though hunters are reluctant
to agree on what will be.

He's coined a new word
for vigilantes who keep a camera watch
on the foothills. He joins them
when he's not writing, and when he is.
He writes about giant eggs,
about a whole new strain.

He brings in folklore
and folk-prophecy. He brings in the date
when the last golden eagle
was glimpsed there. The research is new
and dodgy, but the praise
is as old as the eagle.

Fallon's deliberate use of cliché and the biblical allusion capture the ugliness of the world of the poem.

The State of the Nation

He was saying
they stick a tape across the eyes
before they pull the trigger.
So your man won't see?
No. So that when he dies

those eyes won't splash
out of his head
all over the place. They snapped off
fingers with bolt-cutters
and left a body dying or dead

in an open ditch.
Where? Somewhere
along the border. It doesn't matter
where exactly. At the end of the day
it's neither here nor there.

The eyes offended
and they plucked them out.
A hand offended . . . They cut it
away. And the ring of truth
on the other hand. There's little doubt

they're not only up or over there.
There's men round here as bad
with their blather about Ireland.
Ireland. Poor and lovely
Ireland. They're mad

in the head, brave boys
in the dark, bright sparks
and the blind eye turned.
Draw them out; all they'll say
is, 'Pass no remarks'.

It'd make you spit blood.
If they so much
as shook your hand
you'd have to count your fingers,
limp men leaning on the crutch

of a crippled history.
And maybe they only drove a lorry
with nitrogen bags
on a dummy run to an arms dump
in a disused quarry

or gestured at a funeral
or touted *An Phoblacht*
in a decent pub.
If their day comes
the country's fucked.

Too much, too long,
their carry on as if it's playing
or play-acting. And you mean to say
no one knows who they are?
I mean to say no one's saying.

Cealtrach means 'burial ground'. This poem evokes a world of high infant mortality and stern religion, where stillborn and unbaptized babies were buried in unconsecrated ground.

Cealtrach

The children were never told
about those places. The unbreachable
silence of women protected us
from terrible things.
We heard the dread whisperings
and peopled the swarming spaces with ghosts.

Yet we never knew. They buried
unnamed innocents by the sea's edge
and in the unchurched graveyards
that straddled boundary walls. Those infants
half-human, half-soul were left
to make their own way on the night shore.

Forbidden funerals, where did mothers
do their crying in the two-roomed cottages
so beloved of those Irish times?
Never in front of the living children.
Where then? In the haggard, the cowshed,
the shadowed alcoves of the church?

That Christian religion was hard.
It mortified the flesh
and left mothers lying empty,
their full breasts aching, forever afraid
of what the winter storms might yield,
their own dreams turning on them like dogs.

In a poem that captures the strain of exams, the 'Singer' is not only the sewing machine; it is also the poet's voice longing for freedom. Though the bobbin is empty, the poem has been made.

The 'Singer'

In the evenings I used to study
at my mother's old sewing machine
pressing my feet occasionally
up and down on the treadle
as though I were going somewhere
I had never been.

Every year at exams, the pressure mounted –
the summer light bent across my pages
like a squinting eye. The children's shouts
echoed the weather of the street,
a car was thunder,
the ticking of a clock was heavy rain . . .

In the dark I drew the curtains
on young couples stopping in the entry,
heading home. There were nights
I sent the disconnected wheel
spinning madly round and round
till the empty bobbin rattled in its case.

The election of Mary Robinson as President in 1990 heralded a more open, tolerant and pluralist Ireland. Her parents had refused to attend her wedding because she was marrying a Protestant, but as a lawyer and activist Robinson went on to promote and support equality and human rights. The palpable sense of change which Robinson brought about is described here in terms of weather and landscape.

Inauguration Day

For Mary Robinson

Sunrise this morning spread a red carpet
over grey hills where civil war had once
spawned sterile politics. We had canvassed
every townland and bóithrín where votes,

they said, would never change their colour.
Now hedges danced a little where a robin sang
high above the year's dead leaves, in utter
delight affirming that history's plan

for the future was being redrawn. The season
seemed to stand on its head, with buds shooting
along briars. Neighbours among themselves this evening
discussed the day and the weather, concluding

that a change indeed is no bad thing,
that all the signs are for an early spring.

This is the sixth in a seven-sonnet sequence called 'The Age of Reason', in which McGuinness remembers growing up in Buncrana, County Donegal.

St Mary's Hall

It is very dark in cinemas. St
Mary's Hall was no exception. I went
To the toilet. They are waiting. A gang.

I loved the cowboys and the indians.
This day I really was the Lone Ranger,
A masked man. They kicked the shit out of me,

I was that marked man. I did not know it then
I wore the mark-mask. It took twenty years
To remove darkness from my two eyes

And see the light. They're still waiting, the gang.
Their feet, their fists, their spit. Down in Dublin
I found courage to go back to the pictures,

But still St Mary's Hall is in darkness.
Yes, it is very dark in cinemas.

A woman alone in the house during the day, aware that her life is drawing to a close, gets up and takes a last look. In her book *Last Looks, Last Books*, the critic Helen Vendler writes of how Lady Gregory, 'dying of breast cancer, performed her version of the last look. Although for months she had remained upstairs in her bedroom, three days before she died she arose from her chair – she had refused to take to her bed – and painfully descended the stairs, making a final circuit of the downstairs rooms before returning upstairs and finally allowing herself to lie down.' In Eiléan Ní Chuilleanáin's poem the sounds and movement in the first section tell of an approaching end.

That Summer

So what did she do that summer
When they were all out working?

If she moved she felt a soft rattle
That settled like a purseful of small change.
She staggered through the quiet of the house,
Leaned on a flowering doorpost
And went back inside from the glare
Feeling in her skirt pocket the skin of her hands,
Never so smooth since her fourteenth year.

One warm evening they were late;
She walked across the yard with a can,
Watered a geranium and kept on going
Till she came to the ridge looking over the valley
At the low stacked hills, the steep ground

Between that plunged like a funnel of sand.
She couldn't face back home, they came for her
As she stood watching the hills breathing out and in,
Their dialogue of hither and yon.

Michael Longley began writing this poem on the Belfast–Dublin train amid rumours that the IRA was planning a ceasefire. A ceasefire was announced on 31 August 1994, and the following Saturday 'Ceasefire' was published in the *Irish Times*.

Homer's *Iliad* tell of how, during the Trojan War, Achilles kills Hector and drags the body behind his chariot. Old, frail Priam, Hector's heart-broken father, comes to Achilles and begs for his son's body so that he can give him a decent burial. For Longley, 'It is a heart-stopping scene in which the balance of power gradually shifts from the great warrior to the old king.'

King Priam reminds Achilles of his own aged father and how he can still look forward to seeing him, whereas he will never see Hector alive again. Achilles is moved to pity by the old man's grey head and grey beard, and both men break down. It is at this point that Longley begins his poem. Longley once observed, 'Almost always a poem makes its occasion in private', but added 'this was an exception. It is the only poem of mine that has been taken up by politicians, which makes me think that there's something wrong with it.'

Ceasefire

I

Put in mind of his own father and moved to tears
Achilles took him by the hand and pushed the old king
Gently away, but Priam curled up at his feet and
Wept with him until their sadness filled the building.

II

Taking Hector's corpse into his own hands Achilles
Made sure it was washed and, for the old king's sake,
Laid out in uniform, ready for Priam to carry
Wrapped like a present home to Troy at daybreak.

III

When they had eaten together, it pleased them both
To stare at each other's beauty as lovers might,
Achilles built like a god, Priam good-looking still
And full of conversation, who earlier had sighed:

IV

'I get down on my knees and do what must be done
And kiss Achilles' hand, the killer of my son.'

This poem remembers the returned emigrant who – single-handedly,
it seems – brought electricity to Lisgoold, County Cork.

Rural Electrification 1956

We woke to the clink of crowbars
and the smell of creosote along the road.
Stripped to his britches, our pole-man
tossed up red dirt as we watched him
sink past his knees, past his navel:
Another day, he called out to us,
and I'll be through to Australia . . .
Later we brought him a whiskey bottle
tucked inside a Wellington sock and filled
with tea. He sat on the verge and told
of years in London, how he'd come home,
more fool, to share in the good times;
and went on to describe AC/DC, ohms,
insulation, potential difference,
so that the lights of Piccadilly
were swaying among the lamps of fuchsia,
before he disappeared into the earth.

Greg Delanty, 1995

Irish mythology tells of how, after Lir's wife died, his new wife, Aoife, became a jealous, wicked stepmother to his four children. She chanted a spell and all four children were turned into swans and condemned to spend three hundred years on Lough Derravaragh, three hundred on the Sea of Moyle and finally three hundred on the Atlantic. Though exiled, the swans made sorrowful, beautiful music.

The Children of Lir

Today snow falls in swan-downy flakes
    reminding me of the Children of Lir,
    not solely of Fionnuala & her brothers,
    but all exiles over all the years
with only dolorous songs for company.
    The last note of their singing
    fills the air – it is the silence
    of snow slowly falling.

On 9 September 1982, a young man called Declan Flynn was beaten to death by a group of teenagers in a so-called 'queer-bashing' in Fairview Park, Dublin. Pearse Hutchinson juxtaposes that story with the tragedy of Ann Lovett.

Let's Hope

A girl and her child
extinct in a field.
A boy got beaten to death in a park.
They didn't mean to kill him.
They live.
His family say he wasn't.
Nobody meant to kill her.
One morning last year
from the top deck of a bus
I saw the living sunlight flooding
trees and grass in Fairview Park
with light, life, splendour –
as if no death,
as if no hate,
as if no ignorance ever.
Perhaps that very same morning filled
her field of death with glory –
even love: some sort.
Whether he was or not, let's hope
he enjoyed whatever it was,
or just himself, before

they taught themselves
no lesson soon enough.
Let's hope Ann Lovett knew,
before that fear, some joy.

This get-away-from-it-all poem is filled with movement, the movement of sky, ocean and car. Seamus Heaney said in *Stepping Stones* that this could have been called 'something like "Memorial of a Tour by Motorcar with Friends in the West of Ireland"'; it was written quickly and catches 'the sudden, speedy feel of it'.

Postscript

And some time make the time to drive out west
Into County Clare, along the Flaggy Shore,
In September or October, when the wind
And the light are working off each other
So that the ocean on one side is wild
With foam and glitter, and inland among stones
The surface of a slate-grey lake is lit
By the earthed lightning of a flock of swans,
Their feathers roughed and ruffling, white on white,
Their fully grown headstrong-looking heads
Tucked or cresting or busy underwater.
Useless to think you'll park and capture it
More thoroughly. You are neither here nor there,
A hurry through which known and strange things pass
As big soft buffetings come at the car sideways
And catch the heart off guard and blow it open.

St Kevin founded a monastic settlement in Glendalough, 'the valley of the two lakes', in the sixth century. Heaney said the poem was written 'in a generally hopeful key although it intimates that we still have to earn whatever spiritual rewards we would like to reap'.

St Kevin and the Blackbird

And then there was St Kevin and the blackbird.
The saint is kneeling, arms stretched out, inside
His cell, but the cell is narrow, so

One turned-up palm is out the window, stiff
As a crossbeam, when a blackbird lands
And lays in it and settles down to nest.

Kevin feels the warm eggs, the small breast, the tucked
Neat head and claws and, finding himself linked
Into the network of eternal life,

Is moved to pity: now he must hold his hand
Like a branch out in the sun and rain for weeks
Until the young are hatched and fledged and flown.

*

And since the whole thing's imagined anyhow,
Imagine being Kevin. Which is he?
Self-forgetful or in agony all the time

From the neck on out down through his hurting forearms?
Are his fingers sleeping? Does he still feel his knees?
Or has the shut-eyed blank of underearth

Crept up through him? Is there distance in his head?
Alone and mirrored clear in love's deep river,
'To labour and not to seek reward,' he prays,

A prayer his body makes entirely
For he has forgotten self, forgotten bird
And on the riverbank forgotten the river's name.

Sinéad Morrissey, 1996

Morrissey, born in Portadown in 1972, lived in Belfast through the Troubles, during which the Europa Hotel was bombed twenty-eight times.

Europa Hotel

It's a hard truth to have to take in the face –
You wake up one morning with your windows
Round your ankles and your forehead billowing smoke;
Your view impaired for another fortnight
Of the green hills they shatter you for.

Cill Maoilchéadair on Slea Head is today a ruined twelfth-century Romanesque church with a cross, sundial and Ogham stone in the churchyard. The lives of the 'foreigners in waterproofs in primary colours' are a world apart from those of 'past believers', but the speaker imagines what some medieval scribe saw in this very place centuries ago.

Kilmalkedar Church, County Kerry

Unmortared stone. Uneasy weather.

A knot of calves lain in the grass –
black and white, not long born –
the ruined church with the roof that was built out of stone,
foreigners in waterproofs in primary colours.

Purple loosestrife, purple thistles,
the red-tipped darkness of the fuchsia hedge,
little fields that run down to the sea,
dun wrens, a twelfth-century priest's house, its two rooms,

the spring well by the door, the pale damp day.
And I think did some scribe see
calves laced like these, for his text?
What was the topography of his faith?

What was his weather?
Can we be measured in the lives
of past believers?
Is it for this that we clamber the fallen stones,

then stand, the inspection done, the visit unfinished?
For something still lurks of them here,
some gleam in the day,
a snag of prayers in the grass, a half-remembered threading

of men and women along the thin path
from the church by the shore
to the church on the hill's green shoulder.
Vigil, informed by the whiteness of daylight,
ice to be broken at the well on winter mornings.

And I know we can never be still or simple enough
for what they have left behind them:
a small strong vision snarled on a net of fields.

What does it take to be Irish? Campbell humorously suggests that a miserable childhood is the deciding factor.

Testing the Green

You know that conversation you have
in the middle of the night
when the hotel porter is still serving
about who is more Irish than whom.
It begins with where you are from
and if you remember the '54 final
when Bannon's goal was disallowed.
Then whether you've milked by hand
or saved turf
or lapped hay into the night,
and used you serve mass?
With the last drink, you discuss that wrench
you feel when you hear James Galway
piping from a bar in New York or Perth
and you try for the words of 'The Croppy Boy'.
Once you've that sung there's no more to be said
but there's always one who wants the last word –
Ah, but did you have to walk
the five long miles to school
in the pissing rain in your bare feet?

On 2 May 1997, presenting *The Late Late Show*, Gay Byrne phoned a woman to tell her she was in with a chance of winning a big prize, only to be told by the woman's mother that her daughter, who had entered the competition, had died after posting the entry. Byrne handled the situation with sensitivity, and Brendan Kennelly's contribution that evening helped to bring some comfort to a heart-breaking, heart-stopping moment. He spoke his new poem 'Begin'. Kennelly was once asked what was the lowest point in his life. 'I don't think like that,' he replied. 'I like that old Kerry saying: "Once you get up in the morning and stick your old leg out, you should be grateful."'

Begin

Begin again to the summoning birds
to the sight of light at the window,
begin to the roar of morning traffic
all along Pembroke Road.
Every beginning is a promise
born in light and dying in dark
determination and exaltation of springtime
flowering the way to work.
Begin to the pageant of queuing girls
the arrogant loneliness of swans in the canal
bridges linking the past and future
old friends passing through with us still.
Begin to the loneliness that cannot end
since it perhaps is what makes us begin,
begin to wonder at unknown faces

at crying birds in the sudden rain
at branches stark in the willing sunlight
at seagulls foraging for bread
at couples sharing a sunny secret
alone together while making good.
Though we live in a world that dreams of ending
that always seems about to give in
something that will not acknowledge conclusion
insists that we forever begin.

George Eliot's *Middlemarch* concludes: '. . . that things are not so ill with you and me as they might have been, is half owing to the number who lived faithfully a hidden life, and rest in unvisited tombs.' A similar idea is at work in Mary O'Donnell's poem, with its catalogue of fifteen heroic women.

Unlegendary Heroes

> *Life passes through places.*
> – P. J. Duffy, *Landscapes*
>   *of South Ulster*

Patrick Farrell, of Lackagh, who was able to mow
        one acre and one rood Irish in a day.
Tom Gallagher, Cornamucklagh, could walk 50
        Irish miles in one day.
Patrick Mulligan, Cremartin, was a great oarsman.
Tommy Atkinson, Lismagunshin, was very good at
        highjumping – he could jump six feet high.
John Duffy, Corley, was able to dig half an Irish acre
        in one day.
Edward Monaghan, Annagh, who could stand on his
        head on a pint tumbler or on the riggings of a house.
                – 1938 folklore survey to record the local people
                who occupied the South Ulster parish landscape

Kathleen McKenna, Annagola,
who was able to wash a week's sheets, shirts
　　and swaddling, bake bread and clean the house
　　　　all of a Monday.

Birdy McMahon, of Faulkland,
walked to Monaghan for a sack of flour two days before
　　her eighth child was born.

Cepta Duffy, Glennan,
very good at sewing – embroidered a set of vestments
　　in five days.

Mary McCabe, of Derrynashallog,
who cared for her husband's mother in dotage,
　　fed ten children,
the youngest still at the breast during hay-making.

Mary Conlon, Tullyree,
who wrote poems at night.

Assumpta Meehan, Tonygarvey,
saw many visions and was committed to the asylum.

Martha McGinn, of Emy,
who swam Cornamunden Lough in one hour and a quarter.

Marita McHugh, Foxhole,
whose sponge cakes won First Prize at Cloncaw Show.

Miss Harper, Corley,
female problems rarely ceased, pleasant in ill-health.

Patricia Curley, Corlatt,
whose joints ached and swelled though she was young,
who bore three children.

Dora Hueston, Strananny,
died in childbirth, aged 14 years,
last words 'Mammy, O Mammy!'

Rosie McCrudden, Aghabog,
noted for clean boots, winter or summer,
often beaten by her father.

Maggie Traynor, Donagh,
got no breakfasts, fed by the nuns, batch loaf with jam,
the best speller in the school.

Phyllis McCrudden, Knockaphubble,
who buried two husbands, reared five children
and farmed her own land.

Ann Moffett, of Enagh,
who taught people to read and did not charge.

The hill country of south Armagh was a notoriously dangerous place during the Troubles; according to RUC records, between 1970 and 1997, 1,255 bombs were planted and 1,158 shootings occurred within a radius of ten miles. Lysaght's poem meditates on the relationship between the natural and the manmade in this contested territory.

The Flora of County Armagh

There are new flowers
in the hills of south Armagh,
new army towers
with revolving radar.

The deep-coloured stems
of the willow-herbs make them greater
than the plant in my garden.
These, and other slovenly species

sprawl about the base
of those igneous ridges.
Botany brings me north
for only the second time,

to name the flora
in the famous northern line:
how they fill the hedges of native
farms, and clog up ditches,

with the stamens of radar
on the new ones above
turning on themselves eternally.
Unloved, unloved, unloved.

In a characteristically playful and obsessional poem, Muldoon explores the full range of hand-related metaphors and clichés. The title refers to the old rhyme in which 'They that wash on Thursday/wash for very shame'.

They That Wash on Thursday

She was such a dab hand, my mother. Such a dab hand
at raising her hand
to a child. At bringing a cane down across my hand
in such a seemingly offhand
manner I almost have to hand
it to her. 'Many hands,'
she would say, 'spoil the broth.' My father took no hand
in this. He washed his hands
of the matter. He sat on his hands.
So I learned firsthand
to deal in the off-, the under-, the sleight-of-hand,
writing now in that great, open hand
yet never quite showing my hand.
I poured myself a drink with a heavy hand.
As for the women with whom I sat hand-in-hand
in the Four-in-Hand,
as soon as they were eating out of my hand
I dismissed them out of hand.
Then one would play into my hands –
or did she force my hand? –
whose lily-white hand
I took in marriage. I should have known beforehand

it wouldn't work. 'When will you ever take yourself in hand?'
'And give you the upper hand?'
For things were by now completely out of hand.
The show of hands
on a moonlit hill under the Red Hand.
The Armalite in one hand
and the ballot box in the other. Men dying at hand.
Throughout all of which I would hand
back to continuity as the second hand
came up to noon. 'On the one hand . . .
On the other . . .' The much-vaunted even hand
of the BBC. Though they'd pretty much given me a free hand
I decided at length to throw in my hand
and tendered my resignation 'by hand'.
I was now quite reconciled to living from hand
to mouth. (Give that man a big, big hand.)
My father was gone. My mother long gone. Into Thy hands,
O Lord . . . Gone, too, the ink-stained hands
of Mary Powers. Now I'd taken another lily-white hand
put in by the hole of the door. A hand
no bigger than a cloud. Now she and I and the child of my
    right hand
stand hand in hand,
brave Americans all, and I know ('The bird in the hand
is the early bird . . .') that the time is at hand
for me to set my hand
to my daughter's still-wet, freehand
version of the Muldoon 'coat of arms' that came to hand
in a heraldry shop on Nassau Street – on a green field a white
    hand.

A native of Newry, County Down, and sometime resident of York, Oxford and Poland, McCabe imagines a life he has never lived in an Irish-speaking part of Donegal.

In Donegal

A life can be haunted by what it never was
                        – Louis MacNeice

An irrecoverable future
slaps me on the back
even as another, towering
wave prepares to break

and I picture a life
I never lived, here in Donegal –
a boiling sea, an endless strand,
the slated roof of Errigal –

lived in another language,
in Teelin, Fahan, Port na Blagh,
a fisherman busy by a pier
day in, day out, gach lá, gach lá.

Bolger's poem remembers an Ireland in which a new nexus between business and politics was making itself felt. By the time the poem was published, the sins and shortcomings of the men in mohair had become much clearer.

Ireland: 1967

Nothing much happened around here back then:
The young were an array of foreign stamps
Illuminating the mantelpiece of lonely men
Waiting for crops, death or drainage grants.

But occasionally men would crane their necks
At the distant drone of helicopter blades
Soaring against the sun, in a glinting speck

Of hope that sods might be turned, bricks laid
By Brylcreemed Gods stepping from Mercs
To conjure factories and sink mine-shafts.

The future flew beyond them, immeasurably perfect:
They could imagine his mohair suit and handclasp,
As they gazed, gape-mouthed, convincing themselves
That the Minister himself had just swept past.

Lucy Brennan was born in County Cork but has lived most of her life in Ontario. Here she evokes the suspicion and disapproval that the returning emigrant must sometimes face.

Bridge Street

You went away somewhere – foreign, he said,
as he told me where I'd lived over fifty years before.
No, 'twas in that house there! he insisted.

He still lives two doors down, he tells me,
owns half the draper store beyond.
The mill is gone and the power house
replaced with a library. He's off up there
to read a book, when he stops to ask me
am I here to make a bid on the old bank premises
for sale opposite. A fine excuse for a talk.

Beginnings, that's what I was after.
And we stood in the sunlit road,
memories flooding into me
off his West Cork tongue,
a white-haired man who'd played there
with the child I had forgotten.
And I stayed to watch him go.

No 'twas in that house there you lived!
And thinking I might have heard a subtle reproach:
You went away somewhere – foreign.

Conor O'Callaghan views the oldest part of his native Dundalk in both an historical and a contemporary light.

Seatown

Sanctuary of sorts for the herons all day yesterday
waiting for the estuary to drain and this evening
for two lights queuing like crystal at the top of the bay.

Last straw for the panel beaters only just closed down
and the dole office next to the barracks and the gold
of beer spilled on the pavements of Saturday afternoon.

Home from home for the likes of us and foreign boats
and groups with oilskins and unheard-of currencies
in search of common ground and teenage prostitutes.

Reclaimed ward of bins left out a week and dogs in heat
and the fragrance of salt and sewage that bleeds
into our garden from the neap-tide of an August night.

Poor man's Latin Quarter of stevedores and an early house
and three huge silos swamped by the small hours
and the buzz of joyriders quite close on the bypass.

Time of life to settle for making a fist of love
and glimpsing new dawns and being caught again
and waking in waves with all the sheets kicked off.

Point of no return for the cattle feed on the wharves
and the old shoreline and the windmill without sails
and time that keeps for no one, least of all ourselves.

May its name be said for as long as it could matter.
Or, failing that, for as long as it takes the pilot
to negotiate the eight kilometres from this to open water.

At the height of the 1996 epidemic of bovine spongiform enceph-
alopathy, familiarly known as Mad Cow Disease, 25,000 cattle per week
were destroyed in Ireland.

BSE

On all sides of the open field lies terror,
the self you meet no matter where you run,
the empty sky your gone mind's perfect mirror.
We watch the wellied vet prepare his gun

and slip up from behind on your shy bulk.
The frail cords of lucidity cannot hold,
your teats still bulging with their useless milk
as the addled brain absorbs the mercy bolt.

Richard, Mark and Jason Quinn, brothers aged 10, 9 and 7 respectively, were killed in an Ulster Volunteer Force firebomb attack on their home in Ballymoney, County Antrim, on 12 July 1998. Their parents were Roman Catholic, but after the parents separated the boys and their mother, Chrissie, moved into the mainly loyalist Carnany Estate with Chrissie's Protestant boyfriend. The night before they were killed, the Quinn boys participated in a quintessentially Ulster loyalist pageant, helping to build the Eleventh Night bonfire. They were buried, side by side, following a Requiem Mass in their grandmother's parish.

July Twelfth

I woke this
morning
after three hours sleep
to hear the news
and felt the breath
of evil
in my house

In
Ballymoney
in the night
three children
firebombed
burnt to death:

the Devil walked
abroad
among the drums
and preachers'
talk

incited madmen
in the blood
and dark
this hateful week
of rhetoric
to leave
a dirty smoke-stained wall
his monument:
three children
inside
burnt to death

and what can I do
but name them
say
their names again
for meaning:

Richard
Mark and
Jason Quinn

that they were here
as we
identical
and various

may
this preserve us
at the end

      this day
and all our days
from giving up on hope
from giving in
to weariness
despair and weariness

from failing life
through weariness

Colette Bryce – raised Catholic in Derry – here evokes an encounter
between a young soldier and a local girl.

Break

Soldier boy, dark and tall, sat for a rest
on Crumlish's wall. *Come on over.*

Look at my Miraculous Medal.
Let me punch your bulletproof vest. *Go on, try.*

The gun on your knees is blackened metal.
Here's the place where the bullets sleep.

Here's the catch and here's the trigger.
Let me look through the eye.

Soldier, you sent me for cigs but a woman
came back and threw the money in your face.

I watched you backtrack, alter, cover
your range of vision, shoulder to shoulder.

Some Irish people remember their schooldays as occasions of cruelty. Meehan's poem assesses the damage and celebrates the persistence of the desire to learn and to create.

Literacy Class, South Inner City

One remembers welts festering on her palm.
She'd spelt 'sacrament' wrong. Seven years of age,
preparing for Holy Communion. Another is calm
describing the exact humiliation, forty years on, the rage

at wearing her knickers on her head one interminable day
for the crime of wetting herself. Another swears she was punch
  drunk
most of her schooldays – clattered about the ears, made to say
I am stupid; my head's a sieve. I don't know how to think.

I don't deserve to live.
               Late November, the dark
chill of the room, Christmas looming and none of us well
  fixed.
We bend each evening in scarves and coats to the work
of mending what is broken in us. Without tricks,

without wiles, with no time to waste now, we plant
words on these blank fields. It is an unmapped world
and we are pioneering agronomists launched onto this strange
   planet,
the sad flag of the home place newly furled.

In four calm lines, not unlike an altar in shape, Michael Longley hopes that mysterious, beautiful nature will prevail and, in doing so, will restore the spirit.

A Prayer

In our country they are desecrating churches.
May the rain that pours in pour into the font.
Because no snowflake ever falls in the wrong place,
May snow lie on the altar like an altar cloth.

On the day before the date that gives Healy's poem its title, a bomb killed twenty-nine people and injured more than two hundred others in Omagh, County Tyrone.

Sunday, 16 August 1998

In Omagh
on a deserted street just after dawn
there was no one abroad
but some lone cameraman

taking a shot for the news. And at a slight incline
above the piled debris
the only thing still working
beyond his lens

was the traffic lights.
And there, though no car stirred,
the lights went red,
the lights went green,

and red, and green again;
for Stop, though no one stopped,
for Go, though no one went,
nor stopped, nor went again.

Undisturbed by all that happened
the lights still kept urging traffic

through the crack that opened
between ten-after-three

and eternity. And then they went faster,
as if the bomb had damaged time itself,
then slowed again as if somehow they could
go back to normality.

Then faster still, the light for Stop,
the light for Go, the light for Stop,
the light for Go, the light for Stop,

for Stop, for Stop, for Stop.

Caitríona O'Reilly describes a child's response to religious imagery in a time and place – the mid-1980s in Ireland – when a young woman died after giving birth at a Marian grotto and when 'moving statues' attracted thousands of pilgrims.

Nineteen Eighty-Four

Saint Laurence O'Toole meant business
with his high cheekbones and stiff mitre.
Mary wore lipstick and no shoes
so I sat on her side of the altar.

She wasn't frightening at all,
as with her halo at a rakish angle,
she trod on plaster clouds and stars
behind a row of five pence candles.

She always appeared ignorant
of her swelling middle, or
even politely averted her eyes
(and she never got any bigger).

Later on I couldn't look
for fear she might suddenly move.
That year whole crowds of Marys
wept bloody tears in their groves,

making signs with fragmented hands.
And I knew or guessed why –
the worst thing a schoolgirl could do
was to give birth alone and die

under Mary's hapless supervision.
No apparitions in grottoes
or wingèd babies with cradle-cap
for the likes of those.

Between 1845 and 1852, more than a million Irish people died from starvation and disease and more than a million emigrated. In this poem, prompted by an anecdote in *Mo Scéal Féin* by An tAthair Peadar Ó Laoghaire, Boland sees beyond the horrific statistics and tells the harrowing story of a man and woman, a husband and wife who did not survive the worst hour of the worst season of the worst year. It is, in her words, 'a seasoned love story' which has as its backdrop a whole history.

Quarantine

In the worst hour of the worst season
    of the worst year of a whole people
a man set out from the workhouse with his wife.
He was walking – they were both walking – north.

She was sick with famine fever and could not keep up.
    He lifted her and put her on his back.
He walked like that west and west and north.
Until at nightfall under freezing stars they arrived.

In the morning they were both found dead.
    Of cold. Of hunger. Of the toxins of a whole history.
But her feet were held against his breastbone.
The last heat of his flesh was his last gift to her.

Let no love poem ever come to this threshold.
    There is no place here for the inexact
praise of the easy graces and sensuality of the body.
There is only time for this merciless inventory:

Their death together in the winter of 1847.
 Also what they suffered. How they lived.
And what there is between a man and woman.
And in which darkness it can best be proved.

Francis Harvey's two stanzas – from his long poem 'The Ghost in the Machine: A Haunting' – mark the movement from the stark, bare Catholic church of Good Friday to the light and celebration of Easter.

Good Friday

Love in abeyance. Godforsakenness.
Ships of the soul stricken, foundering fast;
the statues shrouded, the altar stripped,
the doors of the tenantless tabernacle
thrown wide open and the church suddenly
bare and Protestant as an unfurnished
room in an unoccupied house with me
praying for the old tenant to return

and for love too and the lights of candles,
an altar fragrant again with spring flowers,
the mystery of veils, closed golden doors,
and the joy of glimpsing the risen Christ
coming down the aisle to show Simon Peter
the prints of the nails in his hands and feet.

The atmosphere in an Irish pub or hotel lounge is known and hailed the world over. Lively banter, friendliness, generosity are supposedly the order of the day. Stanza one matches that description; stanza two acknowledges that 'there's more to it than that'. The colourful descriptions are overshadowed by the disappointments and the realities that, it would seem, inevitably follow.

Passing the Royal Hotel, Tipperary Town

Instinctively, I imagine
what's going on within: raised tongues;
races being rerun;
drinkers, maybe, in wobbly flight;
or a wedding and its burgeonings;
cards dealt for a big pot . . .

But you say there's more to it than that:
the yearnings fraught with wear and tear;
skivvies clearing the mess
of dregs and fag-butts, misguided piss;
mornings after dogged by nights before;
the embers of regret.

Elvis never came to Ireland – but in this poem by Vona Groarke he
does. She can dream, can't she?

World Music

Okay. Elvis is driving inland
in a black Morris Minor
and white studded shirt. What else?
He's singing, of course,

a patch-up job on 'Sweet Vale of Avoca'
and 'When they begin . . .' It's 1974.
He's seen it all. Even today
he's been through Keenagh,

Ballymahon, Tubberclair.
The names are getting longer
and he's flicking butts, like Hansel,
in a trail. He wants out.

But not before his head-to-head
with the Bethlehem Céilí Band
and their full-throttle version of,
of all things, 'Blue Suede Shoes'.

So just when he's coming up to our gate
I'm ready for him with my book and pen.
Nothing surprises Elvis. He throws me
half a smile and a cigarette stub

that I swoop on, almost dropping,
in the process, my crêpe-paper flag
with its red, stapled stripes
and its thirty-two pointless, tinfoil stars.

This is the ninth in a zany eighteen-poem sequence called 'The Life and Miracles of Christy McGaddy'. The setting is Leitrim, where, as Patrick Kavanagh allegedly said, 'they never heard the name Jesus Christ until the fourteenth century', and the sequence features a modern-day Jesus.

The Happiest Day of His Mother's Life

He got a white suit from America for his First Communion.
It arrived in a parcel from his mother's brother in Connecticut
With a white missal, white socks, white shoes and a red rosette.
His father said no son of mine is going to wear white shoes
So they went into town and bought black ones.

In the porch of the chapel Hughie McGovern said
All he was missing was a veil and gloves and pushed him
In with the girls who pushed him back.
Christy cried even though he got seven shillings
And Mrs O'Donnell said he looked like an angel.

He cried every Sunday after for three years
Till his father put the suit out on a stick
To keep the crows away from the turnips.

World-famous and a papal count, a superstar in his day, John McCormack embodied that phrase 'a fine Irish tenor'. His sentimental songs were loved by many, especially by Irish exiles. Rachmaninov told him that he sang a good song well but that he sang a bad song magnificently. For Dennis O'Driscoll, the only good that comes from remembering his intense dislike of McCormack is his remembering how fond his dead father was of him.

The Light of Other Days

I freely admit to having always
detested John McCormack's voice:
the quivering tenor pitch,
the goody-good way he articulates
every in-dee-vid-you-al syllable,
prissily enunciating words
like an elocution-class nun.
And – though clearly not his fault –
the hiss on old 78s is oppressive
as if he had a fog (*sic*) lodged in his throat,
as if a coal fire in the parlour where
those songs supposedly belong
were leaking methane
through the gramophone horn.

Or perhaps that surface hiss
is the dust coating mahogany cabinets,
their Sunday-best hush
of wedding-gift china,

tarnished silver trophies,
inscribed retirement salvers,
cut-glass decanters
that have lost their shine;
the locked parlour gone musty
as the cover of Moore's *Melodies*
(shamrocks, harps and wolfhounds
wriggling their way out
from an undergrowth of Celtic squiggles).

McCormack's mawkish rendering
of *I Hear You Calling Me* nauseates
so much the gramophone could be
winding me up, deliberately needling me,
applying surface scratches to my body,
tattooing my skin with indelible images
from the Eucharistic Congress of 1932
when, for the mass congregation,
he sang *Panis Angelicus* in that
ingratiating way of his, sucking up to God.

Why do I bother my head tolerating
this travesty? Why don't I force him
to pipe down, snap out of my misery
like an 'Off' switch, send the record
spinning against the wall at 78 revolutions
per minute, rolling it like his
rebarbative 'r's before I throw?

Am I compelled to let it run its course,
an infection, wait until the stylus
lifts its leg to finish, because, well,
this sickly song calls back to mind
a father whose tolerance for such
maudlin warbling knew no bounds?
Could he, by some remote chance,
be the special guest expected indefinitely
in the stale, unaired parlour
laid with deep-pile carpets of grime?
Does McCormack's loathsome
voice succeed in restoring
that father figure, at least momentarily,
remastering him from dust?

John O'Donnell, 2004

The twenty-nine who were killed in Omagh by the Real IRA car bomb on a Saturday in August 1998 included young and old, Irish and foreign, Catholic, Protestant and Mormon. One woman was pregnant with twins. The dead were from Omagh, Carrickmore, Buncrana, Madrid, Drumquin, Beragh, Aughadarra, Gortaclare, Newtownsaville. John O'Donnell's poem, a broken sonnet, tells of ordinary people doing ordinary things on an ordinary day.

This Afternoon
Omagh, 15 August 1998

In Lingerie she is fingering a nightdress she might wear,
Her two bridesmaids-to-be skitting beside her. Elsewhere

Schoolboys like disgruntled sheep wait in huddles
To be measured up for uniforms, dreaming of girls

And football, a new season this afternoon as summer ends
Diminuendo in the town. Here is a father waiting for his sons,

A baby cooing in her pram, two women browsing for a gift
As shopworkers count the hours down, not long left

Till Saturday night, out for a few jars,
The raised T.V. showing highlights in the bar

Of games played earlier today by scrawny heroes
The whole world at their feet, not much older

Than the two who've just now parked the car, discreet
That in a moment will bring them all together in the street.

A poem of time past, time present and time future. The speaker knows that he too will become a ghost, but the moments of music-making will live on in memory.

Ceilidh

A ceilidh at Carrigskeewaun would now include
The ghost of Joe O'Toole at ease on his hummock
The far side of Corragaun Lake as he listens to
The O'Tooles from Inishdeigil who settled here
Eighty years ago, thirteen O'Tooles, each of them
A singer or fiddler, thirteen under the one roof,
A happy family but an unlucky one, Joe says,
And the visitors from Connemara who have rowed
Their currachs across the Killary for the music,
And my ghost at the duach's sheepbitten edge
Keeping an eye on the lamps in the windows here
But distracted by the nervy plover that pretends
A broken wing, by the long-lived oystercatcher
That calls out behind me from Thallabaun Strand.
The thirteen O'Tooles are singing about everything.
Their salty eggs are cherished for miles around.
There's a hazel copse near the lake without a name.
Dog violets, sorrel, wood spurge are growing there.
On Inishdeigil there's a well of the purest water.
Is that Arcturus or a faraway outhouse light?
The crescent moon's a coracle for Venus. Look.
Through the tide and over the Owennadornaun
Are shouldered the coffins of the thirteen O'Tooles.

A collection of voices – fragmented, canny, sentimental – creates a picture of London-Irish motherhood.

Catholic Mothers' Monologue

Well, it's the best education there is, it's the discipline.
If I had a million pounds I wouldn't pick any other school.
Well, maybe if I had the money, maybe that school in
    Hampstead.
Oh Father, when we sang *Be Thou My Vision!*
Don't let her think there's a choice about it. Jesus, if you start
    off with her thinking that she can get away with not going to
    Mass, God alone knows where she'll end up!
I just get Jack into that pew, come hell or high water. I give
    him a big tube of Pringles, it keeps him quiet and by the
    time he's worked his way down through them, Mass is
    nearly over.
You see, you have peace of mind, you know they're getting the
    best education.
Well, as Eamon said to me the other night, no one talks about
    the good Christian Brothers.
Of course there is, there's nothing like seeing your daughter
    coming down the aisle in her First Holy Communion dress,
    isn't that right, Father?
Father Flynn with his fecking sandwiches, they think we've
    nothing else to do. Just because we want to get into the school.
Margaret is down in the centre every Sunday, roasting
    chickens for winos, just because she wants to get the son in
    before he gets stabbed at the Comprehensive.

And they're determined to make an accountant of him anyway and why wouldn't they?

So, well, we were determined to find out if she was bringing her to Mass in London and when we brought her up to the cloakroom, Patsy asked and the child didn't know what Mass was.

If she was bringing the child to Mass, they wouldn't have half the problems they have.

So they are driving around in their Volvos with boots full of drink. That was bought by the funds, drinking the funds. In their big Volvos!

It would make you mad.

And it's their children who get to be serving on the altar.

It's no trouble, Father, so like ten rounds of ham and ten rounds of egg, will that be enough?

Well, Kathleen is a teacher, she knows what is suitable for a child and it's not all this spoiling. She told me herself what she would do.

Isn't it desperate? As if it was bad enough with the pair of them split up, but those grandparents will never see her coming down the aisle in a white Communion dress.

In any kind of white dress, probably. And never see an altar again, either.

It's the grandparents who suffer the most and I'd know being a grandmother.

Ah, it's very sad, but, as I said, if there's alcohol involved. There isn't a chance. Pity, she waited until she was nearly forty.

So they stole the funds and now Father Tim is all over the
tabloids and to think I was down there clearing his garden
for him, yes Father and No Father and himself and the
secretary at it the whole time.

I nearly had a hernia getting into that school.

What's she going to do now she's taken the child out?

But it's a shame, it's a shame, half of it is they can't be
bothered to put themselves out. Too lazy to go to Mass.

I had to pay Aisling two pounds a week to get her to go to the
Communion classes and I couldn't even tell you how much
the dress cost.

But now we have the video and no one can take that away
from us.

I burst into tears when I heard the organ starting up *Be Thou
My Vision* and didn't I start off again at the reception? I
couldn't help it when Father Flynn thanked me again for the
sandwiches in front of everybody.

This is a poem that tells it backwards, undoing the Northern atrocities in twelve lines. If only.

Progress

They say that for years Belfast was backwards
and it's great now to see some progress.
So I guess we can look forward to taking boxes
from the earth. I guess that ambulances
will leave the dying back amidst the rubble
to be explosively healed. Given time,
one hundred thousand particles of glass
will create impossible patterns in the air
before coalescing into the clarity
of a window. Through which, a reassembled head
will look out and admire the shy young man
taking his bomb from the building and driving home.

The Nuns. The Brothers. The Priests. For generations they played a huge role in the education of a nation. They were kind; they were strict; they were encouraging; they were abusive; they were empowering; they were condescending; they were liberating; they were narrow-minded. De Fréine's poem tells of the strict maintenance of a culture of shame.

Post No Bills

As each holiday approached the head nun
at assembly announced in decreasing
digits the number of girls in each year
whose book bills weren't paid – girls with rich absent-
minded parents and others such as Bree

who waited for the tap on the shoulder –
the summons to the office, the demand
for cash, and reminder of the convent's
bounty in granting her a scholarship.

At each such time she studied in detail
the toecaps of her shoes, relieved they weren't
made of patent leather or she'd be
upbraided also for the double mirror image
of her far-from-new underwear.

Bryce, who was eleven in 1981, the year of IRA hunger strikes, grew up in the Bogside of Derry, and has said that the Troubles played out 'on our doorstep literally'.

1981

A makeshift notice in the square
says it with numbers, each day higher.
North of here, in a maze of cells,
a man cowers, says it with hunger,
skin, bone, wrought to a bare
statement. Waiting, there are others.

Days give on to days; we stall
in twos and threes in the town centre,
talk it over, say it with anger,
What's the news? It's no better.
Headlines on the evening paper
spell it out in huge letters.

Over graves and funeral cars
the vast bays of colour say it
with flowers, flowers everywhere;
heads are bowed, as mute as theirs,
that will find a voice in the darker hours,
say it with stones, say it with fire.

It may seem that this poem's sing-song rhythm and regular end-rhymes are at odds with its dark knowledge. But Dorothy Molloy, in her last completed poem, faces the seriousness and horror of a terminal illness with extraordinary spirit. It is, in Selina Guinness's words, 'light verse *in extremis*'. Published posthumously, these lines are indeed last words.

Gethsemane Day

They've taken my liver down to the lab,
left the rest of me here on the bed;
the blood I am sweating rubs off on the sheet,
but I'm still holding on to my head.

What cocktail is Daddy preparing for me?
What ferments in pathology's sink?
Tonight they will tell me, will proffer the cup,
and, like it or not, I must drink.

Peter Fallon, 2007

The speaker in this poem has known hurt and pain and loss, but its message is gloriously optimistic. Peter Fallon's farm is located not far from Newgrange, a Neolithic monument older than the pyramids of Egypt, where at the winter solstice the inner chamber is flooded with light.

A Winter Solstice

A low sun leans across
the fields of County Meath
like thirty watts behind
a dirty blind. New year begins to breathe
new life into the ground.
The winter wheat begins to teethe.

The tarmac streams like precious ore
beside wrapped bales bright in the glare.
Crows shake like collies by a puddle
blooms of spray, and they declare –
a boy's voice breaking in the throat
of morning – a prayer

that works to scour the slate
of unimaginable
hurt. We draw breath in the air –
its shapes are almost tangible –
and the breath and sweat of horses
makes a minor mist – beautiful.

And beautiful the light on water
as the age's newly minted coin.
You'd be hard pressed from here
to tell a withered elm across the Boyne
from an ash that's hibernating.
Past and present join

in the winter solstice.
The days will stretch and we survive
with losses, yes, and lessons too,
to reap the honey of the hive
of history. The yield of what is given
insists a choice – to live; to thrive.

The Irish are known as a talkative people, but we know too that talk can be dangerously revealing. Nick Laird, from Cookstown, County Tyrone, explores the way a divided community becomes tribal.

Conversation

You can't believe the kind of thing
my kind go on about, and I in turn can't
understand the way your lot continually

shout, and shout each other down, and eat as if
someone's about to lift their plate and smash it.
I'd point out what we talk about we talk about

because we speak in code of what we love.
Here. Where afternoon rain pools in the fields
and windows in the houses facing west turn gold.

A flatbed lorry pulls out of the lane.
The mysteries of planning permission.
How someone got pregnant or buried.

The local TV listings. Bankruptcies.
Failed businesses. Convictions. How someone
put the windows in up at the Parish Hall.

How someone else was nailed to a fence.
How they gutted a man like a suckling pig
and beat him to death with sewer rods.

Callan, a teacher, reflects on her shifting relationship with a poem that confronts ageing and urges us to let the soul sing.

Sailing to Byzantium with Mr Yeats

Years ago, in the classroom, I set him off
on his voyage, watching with my students
from the far side of a shore, his stick arms
protruding from the tatters of his coat,
and all of us were young birds
keeping a distance while he took
forty minutes to sail out of our lives
and spread new wings on a metal tree.

All's changed, he murmurs now in my ear
while they avert their eyes and long
for the bell to disgorge them into corridors
of flesh, before I step into the boat
with a scarecrow who claps his hands
and sings like a maniac.

Patrick Deeley connects past and present in one simple image.

Muslin

The island woman came ashore on a bigger island,
settled away from the sea. Her Gaelic dried
in her throat for want of answering. Her lore
was shrugged off by the new people. She held to
her shawl. And when the local children
bundled in, she sent them to the shops on small
errands. Unwinding – it always seemed
to take an age, and it always stilled them – her pennies
from a measure of muslin she could trail
to a ship the sea had washed up, sixty years before.

Joe Duffy's radio programme is a confession box, a platform, a soapbox, a sounding board. Joe coaxes, prompts and provokes his listeners to tell all and the nine callers in Branley's poem come at the topic from every angle.

Old Testament Times

For Joe Duffy

One said
It was Adam and Eve in the garden, Joe.
Not Adam and Steve.

Two said
Let Jesus into your heart, Joe.
It'll all be cured.

Three said
And a man shall not lie with a man, Joe.
The Bible says.

Four said
They're all gay in the seminary, Joe.
Every single one of them.

And Joe said
Does the Catholic Church know about that?

I said
We don't live in Old Testament times, Joe.
Women don't get stoned any more, Joe,
except on their home-grown grass.

And Joe said
Next caller please.

Six said
I'm gay and I'm proud, Joe.
And I still go to mass, Joe.
And no one will stop me, Joe.

And what does the church think of that?
said Joe.

Seven said
I'm gay and I'm married, Joe.
And me children don't know, Joe.
A priest said I'd grow out of it.
Me husband's a good man, Joe.
But I don't know.

Eight said
I think she should stay with her man, Joe.
Think of the children, Joe.
And she's made her bed.

Nine said
I met a fella once, Joe.
And he was going to kill himself, Joe,
on account of being gay.

And Joe said
I'm way over time folks.
That's all for today.

This sonnet tells the story of how a Republican and a Free Stater forgot their differences and played together for Kerry against Clare in 1924. Kerry won: 5–8 to Clare's 2–2.

Munster Football Final 1924

Nothing polarises like a war,
And, of all wars, a civil war is worst;
It takes a century to heal the scars
And even then some names remain accursed.
The tragedies of Kerry, open wounds –
John Joe Sheehy on the run in 'twenty four,
The Munster Final in the Gaelic Grounds:
There's something more important here than war.
John Joe Sheehy, centre forward, Republican,
Con Brosnan, Free State captain, centrefield;
For what they love, they both put down the gun –
On Con's safe conduct, Sheehy takes the field.
In an hour the Kerry team will win.
Sheehy will vanish, on Brosnan's bond, again.

Children born in Ireland are given a Personal Public Service number
when their birth is registered.

PPS

Welcome 3755547K
your small head rests
in the arms of the state
your fingers are counted, your toes
registered, your cries
have found their way
to a vault of need, you're
known, allowed for, admitted
though mysterious to us
and as yet unpersuaded
you drift and sway
and kick against the world
but listen
your breath moves in a far drawer
a number among numbers
you shift in your folder
you open your eyes
you fall through the letterbox
and climb the stairs
you float towards your basket
and gently surrender
ah 3755547K
recognised, acknowledged, filed,

let the complex systems
convince, sleep
on the miracle of your name
spilling across the screen,
the long arms of the sun reaching in.

Sheela-na-gigs – mysterious, naked female figures in provocative poses – are often found on the walls of medieval churches and castles.

Female Figure
Sheela-na-gig, White Island, Lough Erne

Mouth fixed
in a wide grin,
puffed-out
cheeks
fingers to lips –
am I saying
something bad?
No! after
centuries of
darkness
I tell
the truth.

Women –
you look at me
and talk about
your 'desire-need'.
I hear a babble,
then your
wisdom.
Fingers to

lips I speak
my need of
you.

Eyes framed
by a heavy ridge
I laugh –
witness
and survivor.

Caught in stone
I celebrate
all who tell
the truth –
over centuries
of darkness.

Meehan has said that this poem refers to 'a small coastal meadow with
an abundance of wild flowers' near her home in north County Dublin.

Death of a Field

The field itself is lost the morning it becomes a site
When the Notice goes up: Fingal County Council – 44 houses

The memory of the field is lost with the loss of its herbs

Though the woodpigeons in the willow
The finches in what's left of the hawthorn hedge
And the wagtail in the elder
Sing on their hungry summer song

The magpies sound like flying castanets

And the memory of the field disappears with its flora:
Who can know the yearning of yarrow
Or the plight of the scarlet pimpernel
Whose true colour is orange?

The end of the field is the end of the hidey holes
Where first smokes, first tokes, first gropes
Were had to the scentless mayweed

The end of the field as we know it is the start of the estate
The site to be planted with houses each two- or three-bedroom
Nest of sorrow and chemical, cargo of joy

The end of dandelion is the start of Flash
The end of dock is the start of Pledge
The end of teasel is the start of Ariel
The end of primrose is the start of Brillo
The end of thistle is the start of Bounce
The end of sloe is the start of Oxyaction
The end of herb robert is the start of Brasso
The end of eyebright is the start of Persil

Who amongst us is able to number the end of grasses
To number the losses of each seeding head?

                  I'll walk out once
Barefoot under the moon to know the field
Through the soles of my feet to hear
The myriad leaf lives green and singing
The million million cycles of being in wing

That – before the field become map memory
In some archive on some architect's screen
I might possess it or it possess me
Through its night dew, its moon-white caul
Its slick and shine and profligacy
In every wingbeat in every beat of time

A football final from Croke Park on a September Sunday, this poem
suggests, once had the power to raise the dead.

The Final, Galway v. Kerry
All Ireland Football Final, Croke Park, Dublin, 1964

September sunshine, three o'clock,
the last Sunday of the month
and the great stadium
tense as the centre of an atom.

Irishmen in frenzies of isolation
shin up electricity poles
in Camden Town and Cricklewood
with coat-hanger aerials and battery radios,

wild attempts to snatch the faint transmission
from the city's begrudging air.
Later, around tables swamped with beer,
they will talk excitedly of old Connemara men,

dead this fifty years but up tonight
from their brambled graves and sitting
on granite rocks at the gable end
of roofcaved cottages,

anxiously watching the bothereen,
waiting for someone,
a traveller maybe or a youth with a car,
to bring them the wonderful news.

An Irish poem to end all Irish poems? McGovern playfully casts an eye on various versions of Ireland.

The Irish Poem Is

a Táin Bó, a Spring Show, a video
a trodden dream, a parish team, a tax-break scheme
a prison cell, an Angelus bell, a clientele
a brinded cow, a marriage vow, a domestic row
a tattered coat, a puck goat, a telly remote
a game of tig, a slip jig, a U2 gig
a restored tower, a Holy Hour, a pressure shower
a ticking clock, a summer frock, a shock-jock
a hazel wand, a dipping pond, a page 3 blonde
a canal bank, a returned Yank, a septic tank
a green flag, a Child of Prague, a Prada bag
a whispering sea, a Rose of Tralee, a transfer fee
a disused shed, a settle bed, a Club Med
a long strand, a céilí band, a one night stand
a 'barbaric yawp', a sweet shop, an alcopop
a flax dam, a high pram, an email spam,
a new estate, a blind date, a security gate
a pint of plain, a lover's lane, a place in Spain
a cold eye, a bittern cry, a heroin high
a Raglan Road, a tractor load, a Da Vinci code
a lake isle, a wooden stile, a paedophile
a night feed, a Rosary bead, a corporate greed
a lonely impulse, a bag of dulse, a fading pulse

a herring shoal, a fox stole, a death toll
a Pangur Bán, a paraffin can, a fake tan
a fire-king, a fairy ring, a bling-bling
a tickled trout, a boy scout, a ticket tout
a wild swan, a frogspawn, a roll-out lawn
a lost tribe, a Tara Street scribe, a planning bribe
a huge rose, a garden of repose, a wine nose
a hedgehog, a peat bog, a weblog
a whirlpool, a milking stool, a drug mule
a stony grey soil, a three-in-one oil, a Mrs Doyle
a planter's daughter, a school jotter, a mineral water
a potato pit, a banana-split, a gangland hit
a deep heart's core, a Georgian door, a quick score
a newborn lamb, a radiogram, an internet scam
a village master, a sticking plaster, a ghetto blaster
a third light, a second sight, a bungalow blight
a solitary enzyme, a closing time, an end rhyme.

Though never named, the runner in this poem is Sonia O'Sullivan, who spent her youth training in and around her birthplace of Cobh, County Cork. She went on to win a gold medal in the 5,000m at the 1995 World Athletics Championships and a silver medal at the Sydney Olympics in 2000. Theo Dorgan wrote this poem to mark the conferring of the Freedom of the City of Cork on O'Sullivan.

Running with the Immortals

Cobh is a world of silence as the sun breaks over the harbour
and the lighthouse at Roche's Point gleams, a torch
held out to the sky, to the eternal sea.
Something has woken me early, a drum tap, footfall echoing
in the empty streets. I'm at the open window. Too late –
     whoever it is
has already gone by, climbing the hill, steady and sure.

A clear mid-winter morning, frost on the slate beneath me,
tumble of roof and chimney down to the water. Already
the ferry tracking out towards Haulbowline, the world about
     its business
at this ungodly hour – and someone out there running the
     steep
blue streets. Hard work. Cobh is nothing if not uphill
and downhill, the uphill and downhill capital of Ireland.

On a morning like this, a girlchild out early would be thinking
     of glory –

the tall bowl of the stadium, black roar of the crown, the red
    track,
the bend to the straight, the finish just visible through the
    haze.
Easy to dream of gold, olive-wreath, ceremony and applause,
the tricolour snapping to the arc-lights overhead, brass blaze
    of trumpets –
harder to rise to these winter mornings, these punishing hills,

yet somebody's up and out there, out there unseen and
    unknown,
climbing and falling with the street, breath raw in her throat,
pushing towards the sun, pushing against a wall of cold.
Bells from the Cathedral break over the waking town
while she keeps running on self-belief into the dawn,
an ordinary girl, head down, keeping time with her shadow.

I turn my face to the climbing sun, remembering another
    world,
a tall girl surging to the line. I want to find that child's soul
    and say:
Talent is not enough, belief is not enough in this world;
you must push out into the lonely place where it all falls
    away –
and then, if you're lucky and blessed, the friend at your
    shoulder,
keeping pace, will be long-legged clear-eyed Artemis herself.

For John Millington Synge sailing to Inis Meáin, the middle of the three
Aran Islands, gave him 'a moment of exquisite satisfaction'; he found
himself 'moving away from civilisation'.

Immram: Inis Meáin

The immensity of sky,
its murmuring reflection
in flagstone rock-pools.

No verticals to speak of,
only poles holding power-lines,
an occasional person

moving on the horizon.
The whole day
talks to me from the sky.

On Monday, 13 November 1815, at 10 o'clock in the morning, over 20,000 turned up to see Dan Donnelly, a carpenter and heavyweight boxing champion, fight the English challenger George Cooper in a bare-knuckle boxing match in the Curragh of Kildare. A ballad tells of the fight; an obelisk marks the spot. Pat Galvin's poem, in a series of leisurely images, reflects upon how little people know of what happened in that very place two hundred years ago.

Donnelly's Hollow

The earth here holds more
than just the droppings of sheep
or the slow flowering of furze.
At sunrise the canter of horses
circling on the Curragh
is the only sound to be heard

at the edge of the hollow.
By afternoon, especially at weekends
the air can be filled with child-noise.
Over there the whistle of nine-irons,
behind me the whine and rattle of engines
and today's adventurers; leathers, goggles,

scarves nonchalantly whipping the air.
The muffled sound of practice guns
reaches from beyond the trees.
Six months after Wellington

sent the French reeling at Waterloo
local history has it that in 1815

a crowd almost half the size
of that victorious army watched
Dan Donnelly defeat
the Englishman, George Cooper,
on this very spot.
This evening no army or bustling

crowd disturbs the peace of the hollow.
A few sheep graze and stand
like sentries around a granite monument.
From the perimeter edge
the sun falls behind Allen
and all its own mythologies.

The furze spread like fire
through this common ground
and in that yellow blaze
several thousand wave
and cheer as Cooper,
bare-fisted, battered,

falls to the ground in under twelve
unmerciful and bloody rounds.
Skateboards glide across and up
and down these grassy slopes now.
Only the shouts of children toss
and throw the peace of the hollow.

Parents watch from cars;
doze restfully on reclining seats
as if this place offered something more
than just a stone reminder
around which their children tussle
unaware of their local history

or the fact that this ladle
of ground they play upon
holds human blood,
spilled and held here
as in the hollow
of the landscape's open hand.

Grace Wells goes in search of a quieter Ireland and invites us to join her.

Directive Ireland 2000–2010
After Robert Frost

Slip the constant stream of cars and take the old road south.
Best to go on foot, better it be raining. Let your feet again
know dust, mud, the matter of earth. Lean into the wet bank,
to the green band of hedgerow which as you walk reveals
herb Robert's spark, a glint of trefoil, the slow, intimate grammar
of growing things whose language becomes your tongue,
so that as you reach the dusk hills to climb amid rhododendrons
green and jungular, your mouth is a flower that can brook no lies.

The slope that opens onto heather leads to a monastery
offering rest, a place that fed hundreds in the famine,
feeds you now and would provide a bed, dormitory-style,
had you the time. But you must press on, the weight
of the country's change pushing at your back,
and turning from the pressure you descend
to a breeze stung with the scents of a spreading city.

Stay south, fuchsia now in the hedge, fuchsia now *the* hedge.
You will come to small lanes and small fields,
a tang of seaweed, the sea's siren call reassuring you
this is the way, so when you come to the harbour

and the boat waiting, you'll know to board. Humbled
by the ocean, the salt spray breaking on your mind,
you'll find the patience to reach in time –
too long a time to make this crossing easy – the island waiting.

Land beneath your feet, navigate the harbour path
and you will come to a gable end,
a ruined shop, and reaching up blind fingers
into the hole that is there, stretch for the coin
a boy and his father placed there summers ago,
and turning its silver in your palm you'll feel the salmon
of this country leap between the circle of your hands.

On Census Night 2011, 8,036 Filipina women were registered as living in Ireland.

Made in Ireland

I'm the Filipina nurse river-dancing
down the corridor of the neurosurgery ward,
I don't mind that the neurosurgeon
has never learned to dance.
It's his country. I say dance or die
but it's his country.

I've done my three years, I've sent
the money home, tomorrow
I clean out the bedsit, I'll put
my loneliness out with the refuse,
rinse the tears I've been saving
down the toilet bowl

as the sink is still blocked
and the landlord's painted-on smile
is unlikely to unblock it.
I'll gather up these years of occasional despair
with the dust from under the bed
and fling it all out the broken window
so as not to contaminate the next occupant.

I haven't looked at the most recent photographs
of my children my husband sent me last birthday.
I keep them locked away at the bottom of the suitcase
in case I'm tempted to look. I need to be able to stand,
to put one foot in front of the other.
I'm the Filipina nurse river-dancing
down the corridor of the neurosurgery ward:
it stops me drowning.

Vitaly Kharapavitski, twenty-six, died during a performance of the Royal Russian Circus in Scariff, County Clare, on 28 August 2006.

Aerialist

i.m. Vitaly Kharapavitski

I'd talked us all back to Ireland, a week in Killorglin and a plan
to take shovel, bucket, armbands and an inflatable fin,
a picnic basket and a tartan rug to a different beach
each mid-morning. It was quiet and all worked out, so much
we might have dreamed it and never gone – except
that one day we parked on Inch Strand and ploughed it up
as the tide around us did what it does.

Cooped up inside at night was a different prospect
in a rental no one could pretend was Bali or Venice.
For entertainment, ice-cream vans and posters for a circus,
not exactly an infrastructure. The 'Royal Russian Circus':
20 euro a head. I cursed the Celtic Tiger and paid, cash at the
    till,
wishing briefly I'd stayed, done an MBA and, some violence
to the language, lived it deal by deal.

Every artist looks after his own props. The balloon
'exploded into flames', the cage fell, then the heavy steel ball.
Becoming witnesses, one or two hundred people

thought it was part of the act, fire as magic, whoosh and clatter,
nothing irregular in the mid-air routine.
The reports say he was Belorussian, 26, a clown or
'an aerialist in a clown costume'. And that he threw his wife clear.

We'd seen, in Rossbeigh, pre-show and a week earlier,
hanging around, nerveless and going nowhere an elephant,
a giraffe and, between them, a zebra. Canvas and steel
were shaped into a marquee. And from behind Coomasaharn
glider after glider hung in the sky, coasting away clear to the
    north.
A new bungalow advertised art, another a scuba school
and night-kayaking in the phosphorescent ocean

by which that night, stars and stripes on each enormous brow,
the elephants balanced on buckets like shuttlecocks,
while the giraffe nodded, stately and gawky, and a shabby lion
made his unheard-of roar, still a memory on each nearby farm.
A crowd of method actors, the circus animals, though
instead of a tiger the MC, for the sake of form,
squirted water at us from a flower between acts.

The 'Sadovs' had performed for one year and had one stunt:
in it he couldn't find her, she fooled and hid,
the story so simple we gripped the wooden ringside,
grinding our heels into the matted grass and, would it ever
    end,
opened our mouths like parents as he kept
falling over and out of the hot-air balloon. Over
and over he went, *poor man*, who would throw his wife clear.

Weeks later, and back across the water, I saw online
the Dublin owner of the Royal Russians, or its spokesman,
speak of close-knit community, the harness, the hoist,
and the families of the deceased and bereaved flying over.
It seemed for a while, here, as if things might be as they were,
autumn closing in, a net that at the last moment would come
    apart
taking only the leaves from the trees and the name of the year.

The Skelligs are a pair of rocky, precipitous islands several kilometres off the coast of the Iveragh Peninsula in County Kerry: 'an incredible, impossible, mad place', according to G. B. Shaw, 'a place that takes you out, far out, of this time and world'.

Little Skellig

For Paul Cannon

It is not difficult to believe,
a little, in archangels here
as golden-headed gannets swoop
around our lurching boat.
They are poised
as spray-blown row upon row
of cherubim,
along the ledges
of a tooth of sandstone,
which, for centuries,
has been whitewashed with guano
until its galleries are luminous, clamorous
as New York or Singapore.

The boatman in his yellow coat
restarts the engine and twists for home.
Salt water sloshes across the deck
then one gannet plummets

and there is something
about the greed and grace
of that cruciform plunge
which shouts out
to our unfeathered bones.

National identity, especially the identity of the traditional Irish male, is challenged by recent immigrants.

Ireland Is Changing Mother

Don't throw out the loaves
with the dishes, mother;
it's not the double-takes so much
it's that they take you by the double.
And where have all the Nellys gone?
And all the Missus Kellys gone?
You might have had
the cleanest step on your street
but so what, mother?
Nowadays it's not the step
but the mile that matters.

Meanwhile the Bally Bane Taliban
are battling it out over that football.
They will bring the local yokels
to a deeper meaning of over-the-barring it.
And then some scarring will occur –
as in cracked skull for your troubles.
They don't just integrate, they *limp-pa-grate*,
your sons are shrinking, mother.

Before this, mother,
your sons were Gods of that powerful thing.
Gods of the apron string.

They could eat a horse and they often did,
with your help, mother.
Even Tim, who has a black belt in sleep-walking
and borderlining, couldn't torch a cigarette,
much less the wet haystack of desire,
even he can see, Ireland is changing, mother.
Listen to black belt Tim, mother.

When they breeze onto the pitch
like some Namibian Gods
the local girls wet themselves.
They say in a hurry, O-Ma-God, O-Ma-God!
Not good for your sons, mother,
who claim to have invented everything
from the earwig to the *sliothar*.
They were used to seizing Cynthia's hips,
looking into her eyes and saying
'I'm Johnny come lately, love me.'

Now the Namibian Gods and the Bally Bane Taliban
are bringing the local yokels
to their menacing senses
and scoring more goals than Cú Chulainn.
Ireland is changing, mother
tell yourself, tell your sons.

William Wall, 2011

William Wall paints a vivid picture of empty places, trapped existences and bleak futures in the aftermath of Ireland's housing crash.

Ghost Estate

women inherit
the ghost estate
their unborn children
play invisible games
of hide & seek
in the scaffold frames
if you lived here
you'd be home by now

they fear winter
& the missing lights
on the unmade road
& who they will get
for neighbours
if anyone comes anymore
if you lived here
you'd be home by now

the saurian cranes
& concrete mixers
the rain greying into
the hard-core
& the wind

in the empty windows
if you lived here
you'd be home by now

the heart is open plan
wired for alarm
but we never thought
we'd end like this
the whole country
a builder's tip
if you lived here
you'd be home by now

it's all over now
but to fill the holes
nowhere to go
& out on the edge
where the boys drive
too fast for the road
that old sign says
first phase sold out

Ireland is a land of many shrines – telling of local devotion to a saint or holy person, or memorializing sorrowful events. The shrines Moya Cannon speaks of are created with heartfelt emotion for young lives lost.

Shrines

You will find them easily,
there are so many –
near roundabouts, by canal locks,
by quaysides –
haphazard, passionate, weathered,
like something a bird might build,
a demented magpie
who might bring blue silk flowers
real red roses,
an iron sunflower,
a Christmas wreath,
wind chimes,
photographs in cellophane,
angels, angels, angels
and hearts, hearts, hearts
and we know
that this is the very place
which the police fenced off with tape,
that a church was jammed
with black-clad young people
and that under the flowers and chimes

is a great boulder of shock
with no one able to shoulder it away
to let grief flow and flow and flow,
like dense tresses of water
falling over a high weir.

The Proclamation of Easter 1916 speaks of 'cherishing all the children of the nation equally'. Clancy reminds us that this promise has not been kept.

Indictment

An amorphous cluster high jinks it
through Gardiner Street's
November grime, teenage hands
grasp lurid cans of some toxic
energy elixir, the slim frontrunner,
has a dancer's waist, and her over
lip-glossed mouth spews words fit
for a docker, blaggarding all
and sundry, it's innocence of some
sort or other that the worst invectives
they can think of are faggot, loser, dickhead
and she's swanking, flaunting a too-brief
flush of freshness that has her
crew-cut white-socks and runners posse
bobbing after, gangly ankley cowboys
to a man, in year or two she'll be
skanger, haggard and her band
of merry outriders will have conveniently
wizened so we don't see them swept
in corners. You and I will think it 'Skanger'
before our better nature politically corrects us

on Lower Abbey Street they pass the theatre
with its intelligentsia queuing.
Culture? This is Ireland, welcome
and have you met our children?

A reflection on the gains and losses brought by electrification.

The Moon, the Stars

The coming of electricity to the townland was something
like the arrival of the Magi; lorries turned, with tree-trunks
    painted

creosote, horses dragging them into meadow, across bogland,
with giant reels, as if a giantess were knitting wire socks;

men with curled, gaff shoes, climbed high to string the wires
    out
into Atlantic storms; it was a giant step into the new world
    (and what

were we to do with myrrh and frankincense?). It was *slán*
to the telescopic toasting-fork, *Dia dhuit* to the toaster, closing

of the ice-house, opening of the fridge, driving out the spooks
    and pookahs
from their lurk-holes; soon, in cities, the embrace of moonlight

was no more, the stars disappeared behind the streetlamp
    foliage; time
sped up, conversation guttered; gold coins glistered in our fists.

In the inner city, Dublin youths gather on the street. Passing motorists
are in another world.

The Impact

It is late evening when the shouts
of local boys and girls begin. Across this city
street they shoot footballs, bottle tops,
hot chips from the chip shop whose steadfast
neon light shines opposite my window,
more dependable than summer sun.
Car horns bleat intermittently, or tyres break
to a dead halt, and each time I look out
I expect to see some body flung
far from itself, broken to a new form –
but the cars only ever move on, trailing
coarse words that elicit appreciative roars.
As evening darkens and turns the windows
of vacant houses black, they gather under
the light of a lamp post, blow cigarette smoke
in fat rings that grow thin, imperfect halos.
As the smoke reaches a bouquet of flowers
tied above them on the lamp post,
I wonder if they know what misfortune
it marks – though wilting now, I often wake
to see them blooming. As they begin
to move on, a small boy flicks
the butt of his cigarette at the windscreen

of an oncoming car, his parting gesture.
For a moment the embers flare
magnificently, a cheer goes up
in recognition of the boy, his daring,
the unexpected beauty of the impact.

A meditation on the challenge of overcoming Irish modesty.

Skinny Dipping

I'm Irish, we keep our clothes on
most of the time. We perform
contorted dances on beaches in Cork,
or Donegal; undressing under
not-yet-wet-towels. Worried that any gap
might expose us, lay some body-part bare.
It was the Immaculate Conception that did it;
if Mary could conceive a child without
removing her knickers then by God
the rest of us could undress and swim
without baring our buttocks.
We swam serene in freezing seas,
goose bumps freckling our pale skin.
We lay togged out on wet sand desperate
for the weak sun to dry us, before performing
the contorted dance in reverse. Now as I
remove my clothes, peel them off
layer by layer down to the bare,
a brief moment of unease before the release
of water baptising skin. With a quiet 'Jesus, Mary',
I dive in.

Irish men often emigrated to England in search of work, leaving wives and children behind, sending money but returning home maybe only twice a year. Such is the story of Paul Durcan's couple, now dead and buried.

Slievemore Cemetery Headstones

I

KATTIE CARR 1929–1995

She is my song, my turf-stack, my whitewashed wall.
She is my house in the hill up above me.
She is my young woman facing west.
She is my seashell I place to my ear.
She is my ocean I go to sleep and wake up to.

II

MICHAEL CARR 1929–2009

He is my man across the Irish Sea,
My hero of fidelity, who every Friday
Sends me home his wages to rear our family.
Stepping off the bus at the crossroads with his suitcase,
His cardboard boxes of dolls, a sailboat, a tricycle.
He is home now for good, beside me forever.

For an emigrant, the garden outside the window is Eden enough.

The First Story

The email, telling a friend *we're not too bad considering*
      the state of the world, crosses the Atlantic
with the touch of a key. The leaves of an evergreen blow
      like a shoal of emerald fish returning to the same place.
A cardinal in his scarlet robes pecks the feeder.
      The bells of the Angelus ring from St Joseph's.
The Angel of the Lord declares unto Mary, the infant god
      of my childhood is back on earth again, the one
I've ceased to believe in, the lifebelt that keeps believers afloat
      in the storm of being here, issuing tickets to
the hereafter ever since that garden episode, the tall tale
      of our banishment concocted by some storyteller
who'd be so flummoxed we've taken it for gospel
      he'd say: 'Look around you now. Behold, the garden.'

A reminder that alienation from religion need not close off a spiritual journey.

Church

We'd seen the church a dozen times
by day and floodlit in the evenings,
its lines of crooked sentinels, dependable as centuries;
angled shadows from the well-placed lights.
And so we stepped inside the open gate,
crossing the hoary, frozen grass,
and found, instead of stony elegance,
a stolid building, like a threat,
an ugly sign nailed to the door:
Vehicles parked at owners' risk.

I was relieved by this reminder,
not everything is as it first appears
and we may yet, in spite of all I've done,
achieve the life we set inside our dreams.

The glittering sports stadium on Lansdowne Road was built at a cost of €410 million. But what catches MacCarthy's eye are the old trees that survived the construction.

When the Dust Settles

On Lansdowne Road, right by the new stadium
cherry trees still bloom. The monumental tiffany dome
refracts the heat of the sun, broods
over a street of Victorian redbricks

where old gardens flourish. Mature trees
defy wonders of the boom, promise irretrievable Dublin.
As if this were a first spring, damson, malus, plum,
pink heads reach past the builders' veneer.

The slender 121-metre-high spire erected in Dublin's O'Connell Street in 2003 is officially known as the Monument of Light. Pat Boran's riff catches the many different ways of looking at the world's tallest sculpture and honours Dubliners' tradition of attaching disrespectful nicknames to works of public art.

The Spire

(10 years on)

The spire in the quagmire,
The dagger in the corpse,
The skewer in the sewer,
The single finger up.

The stiffey by the Liffey,
The ace in the hole,
The chopstick stuck in traffic,
The North(side) Pole.

The pin that burst the bubble,
The last tooth in the comb,
The first sign of trouble,
The barbed welcome home.

The spike in the crime rate,
The spine without a back,
The hypo from the Corpo,
The stake through the heart.

The needle in the noodle,
The point of no return,
The stick in the muddle,
The javelin, the harpoon.

The rod, the birch, the *bata*,
The Christian Brother's cane,
The crozier of St Patrick
Weaponised again.

The flagpole flying nothing,
The blade-like glint of steel,
The arrow pointing nowhere,
The raver's broken heel.

Stiletto in the ghetto,
Monument of blight,
The nail in the coffin,
The 'we' reduced to 'I'.

An anxious and affectionate response to a son who is far from home.

Letting Go

For Scott

Though I let you go into the light,
though I stood in airports as barriers lifted
and planes took flight, I wait your call.

And it comes from those exotic places,
Chulabhorn, Ko Chang and Satun spoken
in your new intonation and I
have a whole new language to learn.

I listen to the first note of your song,
for its major-key, its melodic message
from seven hours ahead to seven hours behind.
You sleep in my day and walk in my night,
but sometimes you reach across the world,
coming from there, to here, to now,
only a fingertip away.

And some days the magpie's sighting
brings a double pause.
Your song's note flattened to its minor-key.
I catch the echoed sounds,
push useless buttons, fingers faltering.

Then in the empty kitchen's quiet hum,
I write in blue ink on white paper,
wrap plum pudding in tin foil,
seal it and send it:
a sixteen euro packet of love.

An intimate lyric that artfully references Belfast's shipbuilding history.

Lighthouse

My son's awake at ten, stretched out along
his bunk beneath the ceiling, wired and watchful.
The end of August. Already the high-flung
daylight sky of our Northern solstice dulls
earlier and earlier to a clouded bowl;
his Star of David lamp and plastic moon
have turned the dusk to dark outside his room.

Across the Lough, where ferries venture blithely
and once a cruise ship, massive as a palace,
inched its brilliant decks to open sea –
a lighthouse starts its own nightlong address
in fractured signalling; it blinks and bats
the swingball of its beam, then stands to catch,
then hurls it out again beyond its parallax.

He counts each creamy loop inside his head,
each well-black interval, and thinks it just for him –
this gesture from a world that can't be entered:
the two of them partly curtained, partly seen,
upheld in a sort of boy-talk conversation
no one else can hear. That private place, it answers,
with birds and slatted windows – I've been there.

An encounter, a casual conversation, a story told, random connections and a feeling of being blessed are all contained within this road poem. With its easy, friendly, going-the-road tone, it's a West of Ireland moment to be cherished.

Shelter from the Storms

I was surprised to find an old abandoned car
Sunk into a hollow behind a shelter of rocks.
I thought of Dylan's lines: *We drove that car*
As far as we could, abandoned it out West.
I was singing it still when I came upon Festus
Cutting turf. I mentioned the wrecked car.

'So you have seen my shed, my depot.
What do you make of it? Terrific, what!
I tell you now, there is a grand bit of shelter
In there when a storm comes up out of the hills.

Do you recognise it? It's a Morris Traveller,
A classic. It used belong to my grandfather.
He gave up travelling by pony and trap for that car.
My grandmother hated it: the rattle, the smell, the dust.

They only make the Morris Minor in India now,
But they don't have bogs. Wouldn't you miss a bog?
I hear they think cows are sacred creatures.
I have pulled more cows out of bog holes –

Sacred they may be, but they are certainly dumb.
Now ponies, there's a sacred animal for you.
Sure, when you pass one on the road
You can feel them blessing you with their eyes.'

For centuries, monks lived on Skellig Michael. This poem tells of how people on Dursey Island, off the end of the Beara Peninsula in County Cork, still gathered, hopeful that they would hear the monks at prayer.

Hearing Mass

Even when the last monks had gone
the islanders on Dursey still gathered
at the cliff's mouth facing the Skellig
to hear Mass being said, and prayers
carried in over the Atlantic dark.

They stooped beneath the bare weather,
the vowelled gusts and gull cries
and strained their ears against the tide.
And now I see them in the oratory
standing with their faces bowed,

eyes closed and elbow to elbow,
the ocean sweating through their brows.
Then back again on Dursey where I
sense the cloudburst of an old desire
and come to crouch among those ghosts,

reciting above the downpour
the mouthing hum and drone of memory.
But the Skellig has passed into fog.
The wind thrums like wing-beats
all around and I cannot hear beyond it.

An archival recording of an Irish politician addressing an American audience prompted this poem in which two hoary Irish traditions – pinning shamrock to one's clothes on St Patrick's Day and kissing the Blarney Stone – come in for scrutiny.

St Patrick's Day Address, 1920

I clutch a bunch of wood sorrel in my fist,
unsure whether to pin it on;
I haven't long, the 3 leaves will close down at night.
But how we flatter, how we coax –
even though we know it is a useless gift.
Still we insist on bending backwards
to touch the filthy stone with our lips.
What tradition is this?
Shouldn't we be more careful
who we ask to be our allies?
Shouldn't we be more careful
who we lean out to kiss?

The closing of rural post offices, in order to cut costs, has changed the texture of community life. Dyar has said that he wrote this poem 'for everyone in Ireland who doesn't have an email address'.

Death and the Post Office

The job they're given is fairly simple.
Find the place,
go in for half an hour and discuss the settlement.
Consider, if it's appropriate,
the few antiques: the safe,
the signs, the switchboard.
Glance at the books, the electrics.
Perhaps fill out some forms.
But these aul' ones, these Cathleens, these Annies,
they can be fierce long-winded.
For some of our lads their ways
are just too compelling.

Some accept a drink, some'll have lunch.
We'd a Polish guy who took
a ninety-two-year-old out in the van.
She showed him a ball alley.
Fair enough: dozens of ghosts
and no graffiti. But if you're not direct
about the job? You understand,
we've had to weed out the dreamers.
Immunity to stories, I find,

is the primary quality.
You don't want to be sitting at an old table,
under a clock that strikes you

as fabulously loud.
Or find yourself cradled by the past,
thinking a man need venture
no further west than the brink he meets
in a mouthful of milky tea.
If the archive-harbouring frailty
of the postmistress soothes you;
if her wit grants you the lost farm
and maternity of the world;
if her isolated, dwindling village, a place
without a pub or a shop,
whose nearest decent

sized town is itself desperately quiet –
if these things move you . . .
What I mean is, if you can't meet
a forgotten countryside
head on, and calmly dismantle her,
fold her up, carry her out,
and ship her back
to Head Office, however ambiguous,
however heavy-handed or fateful,
however bloody poignant
the whole affair might seem to you;
if you can't stand your ground

when a steep moment
of hospitable chat and reminiscence
might tempt you to put
your mobile phone on silent,
or worse, blinded by plates of fruit cake,
to switch it off completely;
if you cannot accompany
an inevitable change, knowing
you did not cause these people, these ways, to vanish,
and if you will not sign off
on expired things for us,
then, I'm sorry, but you are not our man.

Despite its plentiful rainfall and small population, Ireland has often struggled to supply clean drinking water to its people. In places where the local authority has not succeeded in this task, residents have often had to collaborate in 'group water schemes'.

The Group Scheme

You carry these things. I knew the house
in question was the home of a lad drowned
in the Moy, in the sixties, and that his
mother had not eaten fish since that day;
they never found a body, the divers, and
I knew she lived alone, though I couldn't
think of her name. But you carry these things.
'I'm two days without water,' Mrs Burke
told me. Burke, that's it. I apologised.
I said pipes elsewhere were giving hassle
and that I'd have a look, tide her over
for the weekend, whatever the problem.
She was firm but chatty, and intrigued
that Callow Lake fed this village and more.
'A farty enough source, for the whole district
to be washing and drinking and the rest,
cattle and cars and windows and what have you.'
'And is it filtered?' she wanted to know.
'There'll be a brand new system going in.'
Her reply to this was cool: 'Ours is not
modern so. Is it even good to drink?'

'It's grand for tea,' I said, invoking tea
as blesser of our nerves, and to eclipse
with wryness the two days she'd been without.
Then I spoke about the purifying sand
and stone system that we had at the *point*
of extraction for years, sidling here
for terms that might downplay the blackness,
the volume of the lake. But now the hole
I'd dug at her door was like my own mind's eye.
It needed work. I strove for greater tact
and less awareness welling in my brain.
She watched me strike the pipes. I sensed
then a son beneath us, sinking or waiting,
disturbed and now dislodged. 'Do I know your
people?' she asked. 'Aren't you Doherty?'
'I am,' I said, fiercer now with the hammer.
'Your father did the search and recovery
for years,' she said. 'He did,' I said. 'God bless
him,' she said. And I couldn't get over her
warmth. My breath was short, in sympathy,
my gut all tight, suspicious of the job.

Omey, Louis MacNeice wrote in his unfinished autobiography *The Strings Are False*, is 'a small roadless island covered with crisp grass and when the tide is out you reach it across the sands'.

Homage to Omey

Afternoon sun on my back,
irregular slap of water on rock,
and then, a skylark.

Fine sand blown over
the hill's top, over the lake,
swans, and the sound they make.

Aquamarine, the colour of the sea.
Nobody to say my name,
no one to listen to me.

Nothing to remember
but the currents' swell and shift
and the island itself;

again my head thrown back,
my eyes shut, clear music in the air
and the smell of sea-wrack.

It is Ireland; it is cyberspace. An idealized boyhood seems to belong to the past.

Porn

At dusk
through a window
a boy in a room
home from school

The room is blue
His Mum picked the colour
Duck Egg, Celestial
'I want a shade
with a nostalgic feel'

The boy
could be you
decades ago
immersed in words
lost in a book

Constructing
illusions. Comrades
of the desert
Elephant gods
The glamour

of jets
A future of girls
in shorts

His face
is rapt above
a touchscreen's light
He can touch
The world. Everything
is in there

Today's war
Ancient methods
of harvesting corn
Porn

A new night's dark

His shadowed heart

The Black and Tans were auxiliary police recruited during the War of Independence to assist the Royal Irish Constabulary. They quickly made themselves despised in Ireland.

Tans

Not one who was there forgets, nor speaks thereafter
of the four who entered, crossed the flags for water
and left without a word, of the mugs they drank from
borne outside and beaten with a hammer into powder.

A meditation on the changing nature of Irish spirituality.

A Spiritual People

The Irish go on pilgrimage
To Santiago now.
They like the sunlit walk
Which is good for the health.

When they went on pilgrimage before
It was nearly always to some place
Where the bitter wet wind
Blew from the north-east,
And where, sustained only
By hunks of stale dry bread
And mugfuls of strong black tea,
They crouched all night
Awake among the rocks
Reciting the Sorrowful Mysteries.

The misery of it all
Was presumed to show their spirituality
As was the intensity with which they prayed
For what was uppermost in their anxious,
Often desperate hearts –

That Daddy would give up the drink,
That Aunt May would be cured

Of the sciatica,
That Jim would pass the exam and become
A permanent and pensionable
Civil servant.
They prayed too that they might get
An uncle's farm,
A corporation house,
A man,
A woman,
That lovely coat in Monica Dowd's
In time for Statia's wedding,
Their new teeth done in time
For Statia's wedding.

Even on the road to Santiago
We do not pray so much now,
Having lost our faith
In the all-powerful Father
Who could change things at a nod,
And in the loving Mother
Who never refused
To ask him,
And to whom he always listened.

But if we did still pray
For what was uppermost
In our anxious, sometimes
Desperate hearts
That you might think were beating
Their wings

Against the bars of the temporal,
It would belong to the temporal,
Not the spiritual world.

The temporal is our sphere,
We know no other.
Whatever walls and halls it may have
We are condemned to our temporal yearnings,
For Statia's wedding
And the coat in Monica Dowd's.

The speaker in this poem is an inmate of a Magdalene laundry, where 'fallen women' were indentured to nuns.

An Education in Silence
For the women of the Stanhope Street Magdalene Laundry

This morning, light spilled into the courtyard
as if God had opened a window.
The light is quiet and can't be herded
from dormitory beds to morning mass –
it shines where it wants,
blushing the stained glass window,
washing the priest's words.

My mother doesn't write.
It's been three years. My hands
crack from the heat of the sheets
as we feed them through the mangle.
The high windows admit one square
of light, on the word *repent*,
and I am silent like the sunlight.

Dorgan, 'disgusted with the nonentities that have drifted into power in this country as opposed to people of passion and insight and intelligence', says that 'if you drew a graph from Wolfe Tone, through O'Connell and Parnell and Pearse and Connolly, down to the present, that graph is a steep descent.'

The Angel of History

In the Parliament house on Kildare Street the lamps were burning.
It was a winter night, the usual slant rain falling.

I had paused to light up a cigarette, to watch the lone Guard
stamp her feet, blow uselessly into her cupped, gloved hands.

In the colonnade of the National Library a man was standing,
a man neither old nor young, his head bare, half turned
    towards

the lights in the Parliament house, the high blank windows.
I saw him reach inside his long loose coat, take out a notebook.

I crossed the road, gathering my own long coat around me,
stood in behind him, looked over his shoulder. He paid no
    heed.

One after another I saw him strike them out from a long list of
    names:
Senators, Deputies, Ministers. One after another the names

dissolved on the page, a scant dozen remaining. I watched him
ink in a question mark after each of these, neat and precise.

He put the book away, sliding it down carefully into a deep
    pocket;
he turned and looked at me, nothing like pity in those hollow
    eyes.

He sighed, then squared his shoulders, lifted his face to the rain
and was gone. Gone as if he had never been. But I saw him,

I know who he was, I witnessed that cold, exact cancellation;
walked on, walked home, thoughtful, afraid for my country.

Between the 1932 Eucharistic Congress and the next one held in Ireland, eighty years later, much changed and much didn't change.

The Eucharistic Congress 2012

The Government of the Holy Grail
Is entirely male.

The promises, in what Dawe terms 'my ghost estate poem', are empty, empty.

Promises, Promises

Over the rusty sky cranes lie idly by
    forlorn estates where grass spikes
through patios and abandoned electrics
    hang like wasps' nests in rooms
and halls that no one moved into after all,
    like the half-lit caverns of office blocks
with the reflected moon in walls of glass.

This devastating poem is dedicated to Savita Halappanavar, who, seventeen weeks pregnant and severely ill, was admitted to University Hospital Galway on 21 October 2012. The foetus had no chance of survival, but Savita was told that it could not be aborted as it retained a heartbeat. She was told it was 'the law . . . this is a Catholic country'. On 24 October the dead foetus was removed. On 28 October Savita Halappanavar died.

Waking

For Savita Halappanavar

The procedure complete, I wake alone.
The hospital sleeps. My fingers fumble
over a new scar, jagged map
stitched into my skin –
empty without and empty within.
I trace the wound and weep.

The only sound I hear now
is the retreat of a doctor's footsteps,
echoing my heartbeat.

A reminder of the strange power of the field in the Irish mind.

Fields

There's a place on the Dublin–Cork line
where woodland opens out to fields within the wood
– two or three,
irregular in shape and secretive in their deep surround,
unperturbed by the sudden pulsing passing-through of trains.
And then they're gone.
I always seem to lift my eyes at just this point in the journey,
signalled by some animus of field
and its possession of me since a child,
for all the fields I have traversed
and loved and lost.

Enda Wyley, 2015

A day of intimacy and ease and release within a national, public one.

St Patrick's Day

Our bed is another world.
We are listening
to our own music,
feel the floorboards shake.

There's the promise of a walk
later, out along the damp streets
to the green copper dome
of Rathmines, scent of me on you.

But for now, our bed another world –
rain dripping quietly outside
from the gutter above our window.
I hear it and count the seconds

before each slow drop's fall –
push your knees away from the small
of my back and cross the white floor,
raise the blind to let light in.

Beyond chimney-tops and sleeping roofs,
the mountains, assured in their own life,
are calling us to get up, to cross streets,
canals and bridges to get to them.

An evocation of Irish insularity during the Second World War – referred
to as the 'Emergency' by the neutral state – and of the relationship
between insularity and emigration.

Neutral Ireland

When the lights were out in Europe
in neutral Ireland we had
the light of kitchen fires, cottage lamps
and the light when lightning strikes
a holy place. In neutral Ireland
we had nothing to lose,
folk-cures were in demand,
stone walls of Connemara
leaned a little to one side,
men in the family joined
the armies of church and state.
In the towns where the same man
buried the dead and sold their land
there were nights of dancing,
afternoons of cheers and chants
and county teams trampling
the playing field grass
and on the shore there was always
someone to wave farewell,
someone whose voice never failed
to shout *Godspeed the emigrant.*

Sara Berkeley's spelling of 'color' is American, but in her pocket she holds, in 'two stones and a shell', a little bit of Ireland.

Famine Cottages

The horses move across the top of the hill
the water's still as stone below.
If I had to let it all in
to the places where I feel at home
I'm certain it would take me down,
I would be undone,
I'd drown.

As it is, there is little purchase
on my surface. Few ways in.
The trees send up their prayers for rain,
the hills color up at the mention of Spring.
This year I have been more than half my life
elsewhere. For so long, I have been other,
insular, foreigner with the buried idiom.

Across the reservoir, deer paths lace the hillside.
In my pocket, two stones and a shell
from the beach below the famine cottages
at Rossohan. We used to row there in a skiff.
Last night, the driving California rain
drove home to me
how far away

those beaches where we played as kids: Dog's Bay,
Inch, Cahirciveen, the dry stone walls squaring off
their handkerchiefs of land. New Year's Eve
nineteen ninety-three I flew across
an ocean and six thousand miles to be
where I am now,
and this is how

I've lived my adult life – away from
my original home, in a new place
with new people, an about face
from all I'd known. This is what I chose –
the airport departure halls, the agonized farewells,
and now these hills, my northern moon,
my predawn birds.

When Eoin MacNeill, Chief of Staff of the Irish Volunteers, heard that a dissident group, led by Pearse, had planned an armed rebellion against the British, he issued a hand-written statement dated 22 April 1916. It read: 'Volunteers completely deceived. All orders for tomorrow Sunday are completely cancelled.' Some Easter Sunday manoeuvres were cancelled, including those in Cork and Limerick, but Pearse and his fellow dissidents went ahead with the Rising in Dublin that Easter Monday. MacNeill's countermanding order did reach Moya Cannon's grandfather in Dungannon.

The Countermanding Order, 1916

And my young grandmother,
what of her?
Was she, too, dejected?
No documentary evidence exists.
My mother, too young, at seven months,
to remember, herself, used tell us,
she heard the horse and trap in the yard again
and could not believe her ears.

What was my grandmother doing?
Did she clear away a half-eaten Easter dinner
talking, distractedly, to her two little boys,
as she scraped jelly from a glass bowl?
Did she mix feed for hens or pigs,
or wonder about bringing cattle in for milking?
Did she pray, or take out her handwork?
Was she putting the baby down for her rest?

Only hours earlier
in the swept farmyard,
she had said goodbye
to her husband of six years,
her exiled lover of seven more,
whose letters had been carried
in steamships across Caribbean
and Atlantic tides.

On this Sunday morning, had they embraced
as he headed for the muster at Dungannon?
– as he enjoined her to bring up the children
as good Catholics and good Irishmen and Irishwomen.

(My mother, in old age, was to remark,
with a raised eyebrow,
Wasn't it cool of him, all the same?)

Now, as the trap clattered in through the gate
and the horse, Rebel, halted in his familiar place,
did my young grandmother wipe her hands in her apron,
did she rush to the door?

Although the rising had been called off,
although the great cause seemed lost again,
did her heart not rejoice?

Acknowledgements

The National Library of Ireland, Bríd O'Sullivan, Dumbarton Oaks Library, Rathmines Library; Michael Longley; Dan and Greta Mulhall; Mary Shine Thompson, Donna Poppy. At Penguin Ireland, Michael McLoughlin, Patricia McVeigh and Cliona Lewis were unfailingly helpful as was, especially, Brendan Barrington whose middle name is Brilliant. His exceptionally sound and sharp advice was much appreciated. My greatest debt is, as ever, to Mary Clayton, whose support, sanity, technical expertise and patience were remarkable as I harped on and on. And on.

The editor and publisher gratefully acknowledge the following for permission to reprint copyright material.

BRENDAN BEHAN: 'Jackeen ag Caoineadh na mBlascaod' le Breandán Ó Beacháin/'A Jackeen Keens for the Blasket' by Brendan Behan, translated by Seán Hewitt in a translation commended by the Stephen Spender Prize for poetry translation. Reprinted by kind permission of The Sayle Literary Agency and The Estate of Brendan Behan

TARA BERGIN: 'St Patrick's Day Address, 1920' from *This Is Yarrow* (2014), reprinted by kind permission of the author and Carcanet Press. © Tara Bergin 2014

SARA BERKELEY: 'Famine Cottages' from *What Just Happened* (2015), by kind permission of the author and The Gallery Press. © Sara Berkeley 2015

'The Countermanding Order' (2015), reprinted by very kind
permission of Moya Cannon © 2011, 2015

CIARAN CARSON: 'Belfast Confetti' from *Belfast Confetti* (1989), by
kind permission of the author and The Gallery Press. © Ciaran
Carson 1989

SARAH CLANCY: 'Indictment' from *Thanks for Nothing, Hippies*,
Salmon Publishing, 2012. Reprinted by kind permission of the
author and Salmon Publishing. © Sarah Clancy 2012

AUSTIN CLARKE: 'The Lost Heifer', 'The Planter's Daughter', 'The
Envy of Poor Lovers', 'Unmarried Mothers' from *Austin Clarke:
Collected Poems* (2008), reprinted by kind permission of Aoife
Clarke and Carcanet Press

HARRY CLIFTON: 'Ireland' from *Comparative Lives* (1982) and
Selected Poems (2014), reprinted by kind permission of the author
and Bloodaxe Books. © Harry Clifton 1982, 2014

MICHAEL COADY: 'Assembling the Parts' from *Oven Lane* (1987),
by kind permission of the author and The Gallery Press. ©
Michael Coady 1987

SUSAN CONNOLLY: 'Female Figure', reprinted by kind permission
of the author. From *Forest Music*, Shearsman Books Ltd, 58
Velwell Rd, Exeter EX4 4 LD. © Susan Connolly 2009

ANTHONY CRONIN: 'A Spiritual People' from *Body and Soul* (New
Island Books, 2014), reprinted by kind permission of the author
and New Island. © Anthony Cronin 2014

TONY CURTIS: 'Shelter from the Storms', reprinted by kind
permission of the author. © Tony Curtis. *Pony* by Tony Curtis
and David Lilburn (Occasional Press, 2014)

GERALD DAWE: 'Promises, Promises' from *Micky Finn's Air* (2014),
by kind permission of the author and The Gallery Press. © Gerald
Dawe 2014

CECIL DAY LEWIS: 'Fishguard to Rosslare' from *The Room and*

300   *Other Poems* (1965), reprinted by kind permission of Penguin
      Random House. © The Estate of Cecil Day Lewis 1965

JOHN F. DEANE: 'The Moon, the Stars' from *20/12 Twenty Poets
      Respond to Science in Twelve Lines* (2012), by kind permission of
      the author and The Dedalus Press. © John F. Deane 2012

PATRICK DEELEY: 'Muslin' from *The Bones of Creation* (2008), by
      kind permission of the author and The Dedalus Press. © Patrick
      Deeley 2008

CELIA DE FRÉINE: 'Post No Bills' from *Scarecrows at Newtownards*
      (2005), reprinted by kind permission of Celia de Fréine. © Celia
      de Fréine 1995, 2005

GREG DELANTY: 'The First Story' from *The Greek Anthology: Book
      XVII* (2012), and 'The Children of Lir' from *Collected Poems 1986–
      2006* (2006), reprinted by kind permission of the author and
      Carcanet Press. © Greg Delanty 1995, 2006, 2012

DENIS DEVLIN: 'Boy Bathing' and 'After Five O'Clock' from
      Collected Poems (1989), by kind permission of The Estate of Denis
      Devlin and The Dedalus Press. © The Estate of Denis Devlin 1989

THEO DORGAN: 'Running with the Immortals' from *Greek* (2010),
      'The Angel of History' from *Nine Bright Shiners* (2014), by kind
      permission of the author and The Dedalus Press. © Theo Dorgan
      2010, 2014

SEÁN DUNNE: 'Holy Well' (from *West Cork*) from *Collected Poems*
      (2005), by kind permission of The Estate of Seán Dunne and The
      Gallery Press. © The Estate of Seán Dunne and The Gallery Press
      2005

LORD DUNSANY (EDWARD PLUNKETT, 18TH BARON OF
      DUNSANY): 'To the Fallen Irish Soldiers', reprinted by kind
      permission of Joseph Doyle and The Estate of Lord Dunsany

PAUL DURCAN: 'Ireland 1972', 'The Cabinet Table' and 'Making Love
      Outside Áras an Uachtaráin' from *Life is a Dream: 40 Years*

Reading Poems 1967–2007 (Harvill Secker, 2009). 'Slievemore 301
Cemetery Headstones' from *Praise in Which I Live and Move and
Have My Being* (Harvill Secker, 2012), reprinted by permission of
Rogers, Coleridge & White, 20 Powis Mews, London W11 1JN.
© Paul Durcan 2009, 2012

MARTIN DYAR: 'The Group Scheme', 'Death and the Post Office'
from *Maiden Names* (Arlen House, 2013), reprinted by kind
permission of Martin Dyar and Arlen House. © Martin Dyar
2013

DESMOND EGAN: 'The Northern Ireland Question' from *Elegies*
(Goldsmith Press, 1996), reprinted by kind permission of
Desmond Egan and Goldsmith Press. © Desmond Egan 1996

MARTINA EVANS: 'Catholic Mothers' Monologue' from *Can
Dentists Be Trusted?* (2004), reprinted by kind permission of
Martina Evans and Anvil Poetry Press. Anvil Poetry Press,
Neptune House, 70 Royal Hill, London SE10 8RF. © Martina
Evans 2004

PADRAIC FALLON: 'Day Ashore' from *A Look in the Mirror and
Other Poems* (2003), reprinted by kind permission of Carcanet
Press. © The Estate of Padraic Fallon

PETER FALLON: 'The State of the Nation' from *Eye to Eye* (1992) and
'A Winter Solstice' from *The Company of Horses* (2007), by kind
permission of the author and The Gallery Press. © Peter Fallon
1992, 2007

PADRAIC FIACC: 'Enemy Encounter', reprinted by very kind
permission of the author and Aodán Mac Póilin. © Padraic Fiacc
1986

JOHN FITZGERALD: 'Fields', reprinted by kind permission of the
author. © John Fitzgerald 2015

GABRIEL FITZMAURICE: 'Munster Football Final 1924' from *In
Praise of Football* (2009), reprinted by kind permission of Mercier

FRANCIS HARVEY: 'Good Friday' from *Collected Poems* (2007), by   303
    kind permission of The Estate of Francis Harvey and The Dedalus
    Press. © The Estate of Francis Harvey 2007

ANNE HAVERTY: 'Porn', reprinted by kind permission of Anne
    Haverty. © Anne Haverty 2014

DERMOT HEALY: 'Sunday, 16 August 1998' from *The Reed Bed*
    (2001), by kind permission of The Estate of Dermot Healy and
    The Gallery Press. © The Estate of Dermot Healy 2001, 2014

SEAMUS HEANEY: 'Churning Day', 'Thatcher', 'Orange Drums,
    Tyrone, 1966', 'Casualty', 'Clearances 3', 'Postscript' and 'St Kevin
    and the Blackbird' from *Opened Ground: Poems 1966–1996*,
    reprinted by kind permission of Faber and Faber. © The Estate of
    Seamus Heaney 1966, 1969, 1975, 1979, 1987, 1996

JOHN HEWITT: 'First Corncrake' from *Collected Poems* (1991),
    reprinted by kind permission of Blackstaff Press. © The Estate of
    John Hewitt

SEÁN HEWITT: 'A Jackeen Keens for the Blasket', reprinted by kind
    permission of the translator. © Seán Hewitt 2012

RITA ANN HIGGINS: 'Ireland Is Changing Mother' from *Ireland Is
    Changing Mother* (2011), reprinted by kind permission of the
    author and Bloodaxe Books. © Rita Ann Higgins 2011

PEARSE HUTCHINSON: 'Let's Hope' from *Collected Poems* (2002),
    by kind permission of The Estate of Pearse Hutchinson and The
    Gallery Press. © The Estate of Pearse Hutchinson 2001, 2012

JOE KANE: 'Made in Ireland' from *Lazarus on the Backstrand* (New
    Island, 2011), reprinted by kind permission of New Island. © The
    Estate of Joe Kane 2011

PATRICK KAVANAGH: 'Inniskeen Road: July Evening', 'Spraying the
    Potatoes', 'Stony Grey Soil', 'A Christmas Childhood', 'Shancoduff',
    'In Memory of My Mother', 'Kerr's Ass' and 'Epic' from *Collected
    Poems of Patrick Kavanagh*, edited by Antoinette Quinn (Allen

THOMAS MCCARTHY: 'State Funeral' from *Mr Dinneen's Downfall:*
New and Selected Poems, reprinted by kind permission of the
author and Anvil Press. © Thomas McCarthy 1981, 1999

DONAGH MACDONAGH: 'Dublin Made Me', 'A Warning to
Conquerors' from *A Warning to Conquerors* (Dolmen Press,
1968), reprinted by kind permission of Barbara Cashin and Niall
MacDonagh. © The Estate of Donagh MacDonagh

PATRICK MACDONOGH: 'O Come to the Land' from *Poems* (2001),
by kind permission of The Estate of Patrick MacDonogh and The
Gallery Press. © The Estate of Patrick MacDonogh 2001

LIAM MACGABHANN: 'Connolly' from *Rags, Robes and Rebels*
(1933), reprinted by kind permission of Dorothy MacGabhann.
© The Estate of Liam MacGabhann

IGGY MCGOVERN: 'The Irish Poem Is' from *Safe House* (2010), by
kind permission of the author and The Dedalus Press. © Iggy
McGovern

THOMAS MACGREEVY: 'The Six Who Were Hanged' from
Collected Poems of Thomas MacGreevy: An Annotated Edition,
edited by Susan Schreibman. Reprinted by kind permission of
Mrs Margaret Farrington and Mr Robbie Ryan

MEDBH MCGUCKIAN: 'The "Singer"' from *The Flower Master and
Other Poems* (1993), by kind permission of the author and The
Gallery Press. © Medbh McGuckian 1982, 1993

FRANK MCGUINNESS: 'St Mary's Hall' from *Booterstown* (1994), by
kind permission of the author and The Gallery Press. © Frank
McGuinness 1994

VIVIENNE MCKECHNIE: 'Letting Go' from *A Butterfly's Wing*
(2013). This reworked version reprinted by kind permission of the
author and Arlen House, PO Box 222, Galway. © Vivienne
McKechnie 2013, 2015

SINÉAD MORRISSEY: 'Europa Hotel' from *There was Fire in*   307
Vancouver (1996), 'Lighthouse' from *Parallax* (2013), reprinted by
kind permission of the author and Carcanet Press. © Sinéad
Morrissey 1996, 2013

PAUL MULDOON: 'Ireland', 'Anseo', 'They That Wash on Thursday'
from *Poems 1968–1998* (2001), reprinted by kind permission of
the author and Faber and Faber. © Paul Muldoon 1980, 1998

RICHARD MURPHY: 'Casement's Funeral' from *Poems 1952–2012*
(2013), reprinted by kind permission of The Lilliput Press. ©
Richard Murphy 2012

EILÉAN NÍ CHUILLEANÁIN: 'Old Roads' and 'That Summer' from
Selected Poems (2008), by kind permission of The Gallery Press. ©
Eiléan Ní Chuilleanáin 2008.

NUALA NÍ DHOMHNAILL: 'Ceist na Teangan' by Nuala Ní
Dhomhnaill from *Pharaoh's Daughter* (1990), 'The Language
Issue' translated by Paul Muldoon, by kind permission of the
author and translator and The Gallery Press. © Nuala Ní
Dhomhnaill and Paul Muldoon 1990

JEAN O'BRIEN: 'Skinny Dipping' from *Merman* (2012), reprinted
by kind permission of the author and Salmon Poetry. © Jean
O'Brien 2012

CONOR O'CALLAGHAN: 'Seatown' from *Seatown* (1999), by kind
permission of the author and The Gallery Press. © Conor
O'Callaghan 1999

JULIE O'CALLAGHAN: 'The Great Blasket Island' from *What's
What* (1991), reprinted by kind permission of Bloodaxe Books,
Highgreen, Tarset, Northumberland NE48 1RP. © Julie
O'Callaghan 1991

JOHN O'DONNELL: 'This Afternoon' from *Icarus Sees His Father Fly*
(2004), reprinted by kind permission of The Dedalus Press. ©
John O'Donnell 2004

Index of Poets

Behan, Brendan *see* Ó Beacháin,
    Breandán
Bergin, Tara, 270
Berkeley, Sara, 292
Boland, Eavan, 120, 192
Bolger, Dermot, 176
Boran, Pat, 262
Branley, Mary, 217
Brennan, Lucy, 177
Bryce, Colette, 184, 210
Bushe, Paddy, 149
Callaghan, Louise C., 233
Callan, Mary Rose, 215
Campbell, Siobhán, 165
Cannon, Moya, 244, 250, 294
Carson, Ciaran, 121
Clancy, Sarah, 252
Clarke, Austin, 18, 28, 61, 70
Clifton, Harry, 110
Coady, Michael, 125
Connolly, Susan, 223
Cronin, Anthony, 280
Curtis, Tony, 267
Dawe, Gerald, 287
Day Lewis, Cecil, 71
Deane, John F., 254
Deeley, Patrick, 216

De Fréine, Celia, 209
Delanty, Greg, 156, 259
Devlin, Denis, 46, 47
Dorgan, Theo, 231, 284
Dunne, Seán, 117
Dunsany, Lord, 26
Durcan, Paul, 84, 94, 118, 258
Dyar, Martin, 271, 274
Egan, Desmond, 81
Evans, Martina, 205
Fallon, Padraic, 43
Fallon, Peter, 143, 212
Fiacc, Padraic, 119
Fitzgerald, John, 289
Fitzmaurice, Gabriel, 220
French, Tom, 279
Galvin, Pat, 234
Gillis, Alan, 208
Gore-Booth, Eva, 11
Gorman, Michael, 130
Grennan, Eamon, 112
Groarke, Vona, 196
Hanberry, Gerard, 227
Hardie, Kerry, 163
Hartnett, Michael, 77, 85, 115
Harvey, Francis, 194
Haverty, Anne, 277

312

Healy, Dermot, 188
Heaney, Seamus, 72, 79, 90, 98, 124, 159, 160
Hewitt, John, 57
Hewitt, Seán (trans.) 60
Higgins, Rita Ann, 246
Hutchinson, Pearse, 157
Kane, Joe, 239
Kavanagh, Patrick, 35, 48, 52, 54, 65, 66, 68, 69
Kennelly, Brendan, 132, 166
Kettle, Thomas, 8
Laird, Nick, 214
Ledwidge, Francis, 3
Longley, Michael, 103, 133, 153, 187, 204
Lysaght, Sean, 171
McAuley, James, 87
McAuliffe, John, 241
McBreen, Joan, 276
McCabe, Cathal, 175
MacCarthy, Catherine Phil, 261
McCarthy, Thomas, 95
MacDonagh, Donagh, 50, 78
MacDonogh, Patrick, 62
MacGabhann, Liam, 31
McGovern, Iggy, 229
MacGreevy, Thomas, 14
McGuckian, Medbh, 148
McGuinness, Frank, 150
McKechnie, Vivienne, 264
MacKenna, John, 260
MacNeice, Louis, 38
Mahon, Derek, 74, 91, 107, 116
Mathews, Aidan, 114

Meehan, Paula, 135, 185, 225
Molloy, Dorothy, 211
Monahan, Noel, 286
Montague, John, 82, 86
Moran, Patrick, 195
Morrissey, Sinéad, 162, 266
Muldoon, Paul, 104, 105, 173
Muldoon, Paul (trans.), 128
Murphy, Richard, 75
Ní Chuilleanáin, Eiléan, 89, 151
Ní Dhomhnaill, Nuala, 127
Ní Ghríofa, Doireann, 288
Ó Beacháin, Breandán, 59
O'Brien, Jean, 257
O'Callaghan, Conor, 178
O'Callaghan, Julie, 134
O'Donnell, John, 202
O'Donnell, Mary, 168
O'Donoghue, Bernard, 122, 139
O'Driscoll, Dennis, 199
O'Malley, Mary, 146
O'Reilly, Caitríona, 190
O'Sullivan, Leanne, 269
Ormsby, Frank, 97
Pearse, Patrick, 1
Quinn, Leeanne, 255
Riordan, Maurice, 155
Rodgers, W. R., 41
Ryan, Richard, 80
Salkeld, Blanaid, 44
Sigerson Shorter, Dora, 12
Sirr, Peter, 221
Smyth, Gerard, 291
Strong, Eithne, 129
Sweeney, Matthew, 141

Traynor, Jessica, 283
Tynan, Katharine, 10
Wall, William, 248
Wells, Grace, 237
Wheatley, David, 180

Woods, Macdara, 181
Woods, Vincent, 198
Wyley, Enda, 290
Yeats, W. B., 4, 19, 21, 23, 29, 33, 36

Index of Titles

Aerialist, 241

After Five O'Clock, 47

Among School Children, 23

Angel of History, The, 284

Anseo, 105

Assembling the Parts, 125

Beara Peninsula, 129

Begin, 166

Belfast Confetti, 121

Boy Bathing, 46

Break, 184

Bridge Street, 177

BSE, 180

Cabinet Table, The, 118

Casement's Funeral, 75

Casualty, 98

Catholic Mothers' Monologue, 205

Cealtrach, 146

Ceasefire, 153

Ceilidh, 204

Ceist na Teangan, 127

Children of Lir, The, 156

Christmas Childhood, A, 54

Church, 260

Churning Day, 72

Circus Animals' Desertion, The, 36

Civil Servant, The (*from* Wreaths), 103

Comrades, 11

Connolly, 31

Conversation, 214

Coole Park, 1929, 29

Countermanding Order 1916, The, 294

Day Ashore, 43

Death and the Post Office, 271

Death of a Field, 225

Death of an Irishwoman, 85

Death of Irish, The, 114

Directive Ireland 2000–2010, 237

Disused Shed in Co. Wexford, A, 91

Donnelly's Hollow, 234

Dublin, 38

Dublin Made Me, 50

Dubliner, A, 44

Eagle, The, 141

Easter 1916, 4

Education in Silence, An, 283

Eily Kilbride, 132

Emigrant Irish, The, 120

Enemy Encounter, 119

Envy of Poor Lovers, The, 61

316   Epic, 69

Eucharistic Congress 2012, The, 286

Europa Hotel, 162

Facts of Life, Ballymoney, 112

Famine Cottages, 292

Famine Village, 80

Female Figure, 223

Fields, 289

Final, Galway v. Kerry, The, 227

First Corncrake, 57

First Story, The, 259

Fishguard to Rosslare, 71

Flora of County Armagh, The, 171

Garage in Co. Cork, A, 107

Gethsemane Day, 211

Ghost Estate, 248

Good Friday, 194

Great Blasket Island, The, 134

Green Beer, 87

Group Scheme, The, 274

Happiest Day of His Mother's Life, The, 198

Hearing Mass, 269

Holy Well (*from* West Cork), 117

Homage to Omey, 276

'I saw magic on a green country road – ', 77

Ice-Cream Man, The, 133

Immram: Inis Meáin, 233

Impact, The, 255

In Donegal, 175

In Memory of Eva Gore-Booth and Con Markiewicz, 33

In Memory of My Mother, 66

Inauguration Day, 149

Inchicore Haiku (25, 37, 55, 82), 115

Indictment, 252

Inis Oírr, 74

Inniskeen Road: July Evening, 35

Ireland, 104

Ireland, 110

Ireland Is Changing Mother, 246

Ireland 1967, 176

Ireland 1972, 84

Irish Lake, An, 41

Irish Poem Is, The, 229

Jackeen ag Caoineadh na mBlascaod, 59

Jackeen Keens for the Blasket, A [trans.], 60

July Twelfth, 181

Kerr's Ass, 68

Kilmalkedar Church, County Kerry, 163

Kinsale, 116

Lament for Thomas MacDonagh, 3

Language Issue, The [trans.], 128

Let's Hope. 157

Letting Go, 264

Light of Other Days, The, 199

Lighthouse, 266

Literacy Class, South Inner City, 185

Little Skellig, 244

Long Vacation, The, 10

Lost Heifer, The, 18

Made in Ireland, 239

Making Love Outside Áras an
    Uachtaráin, 94

Moon, the Stars, The, 254

Munster Final, 122

Munster Football Final 1924, 220

Muslin, 216

Neutral Ireland, 291

1981, 210

Nineteen Eighty-Four, 190

Northern Ireland Question, The, 81

Nun Takes the Veil, A, 139

O, Come to the Land, 62

Old Roads, 89

Old Testament Times, 217

Orange Drums, Tyrone, 1966, 90

Passing the Royal Hotel, Tipperary
    Town, 195

People I Grew Up with Were Afraid,
    The, 130

Planter's Daughter, The, 28

Porn, 277

Post No Bills, 209

Postscript, 159

PPS, 221

Prayer, A, 187

Progress, 208

Promises, Promises, 287

Quarantine, 192

Running with the Immortals, 231

Rural Electrification 1956, 155

Sailing to Byzantium, 21

Sailing to Byzantium with Mr Yeats,
    215

Seatown, 178

St Kevin and the Blackbird, 160

St Mary's Hall, 150

St Patrick's Day, 290

St Patrick's Day Address, 1920, 270

Shancoduff, 65

Shelter from the Storms, 267

Shrines, 250

Siege of Mullingar, The, 82

'Singer', The, 148

Six Who Were Hanged, The, 14

Sixteen Dead Men, 12

Skinny Dipping, 257

Slievemore Cemetery Headstones,
    258

Small Town in Ireland, A, 97

Spire, The, 262

Spiritual People, A, 280

Spraying the Potatoes, 48

Stare's Nest by My Window, The,
    19

State Funeral, 95

State of the Nation, The, 143

Statue of the Virgin at Granard
    Speaks, The, 135

Stony Grey Soil, 52

Sunday, 16 August 1998, 188

318   Tans, 279

Testing the Green, 165

That Summer, 151

Thatcher, 79

They That Wash on Thursday, 173

This Afternoon, 202

To My Daughter Betty, The Gift of
    God, 8

To the Fallen Irish Soldiers, 26

Unlegendary Heroes, 168

Unmarried Mothers, 70

Waking, 288

Warning to Conquerors, A, 78

Wayfarer, The, 1

'When all the others were away at
    Mass' (*from* Clearances), 124

When the Dust Settles, 261

Windharp. 86

Winter Solstice, A, 212

World Music, 196